Macmillan McGraw-Hill

Math Connects

5

Chapter 14
Resource Masters

 Macmillan/McGraw-Hill

The McGraw·Hill Companies

 Macmillan/McGraw-Hill

Send all inquiries to:
Macmillan/McGraw-Hill
8787 Orion Place
Columbus, OH 43240-4027

ISBN: 978-0-02-107286-6
MHID: 0-02-107286-8

Chapter 14 Resource Masters

Printed in the United States of America.

5 6 7 8 9 10   RHR   16 15 14 13 12 11 10

Contents

Teacher's Guide to Using the
Chapter 14 Resource Masters

The *Chapter 14 Resource Masters* includes the core materials needed for Chapter 14. These materials include worksheets, extensions, and assessment options. The answers for these pages appear at the back of this booklet.

All of the materials found in this booklet are included for viewing and printing on the *TeacherWorks Plus*™ CD-ROM.

Chapter Resources

Graphic Organizer (page 1) This master is a tool designed to assist students with comprehension of grade-level concepts. While the content and layout of these tools vary, their goal is to assist students by providing a visual representation from which they can learn new concepts.

Student Glossary (page 2) This master is a study tool that presents the key vocabulary terms from the chapter. You may suggest that students highlight or star the terms they do not understand. Give this list to students before beginning Lesson 14–1. Remind them to add these pages to their mathematics study notebooks.

Anticipation Guide (page 6) This master is a survey designed for use before beginning the chapter. You can use this survey to highlight what students may or may not know about the concepts in the chapter. If feasible, interview students in small groups, asking them the interview questions in the guide. There is space for recording how well students answer the questions before they complete the chapter. You may find it helpful to interview students a second time, after completing the chapter, to determine their progress.

Game (page 7) A game is provided to reinforce chapter concepts and may be used at appropriate times throughout the chapter.

Resources for Computational Lessons

Reteach Each lesson has an associated Reteach worksheet. In general, the Reteach worksheet focuses on the same lesson content but uses a different approach, learning style, or modality than that used in the Student Edition. The Reteach worksheet closes with computational practice of the concept.

Skills Practice The Skills Practice worksheet for each lesson focuses on the computational aspect of the lesson. The Skills Practice worksheet may be helpful in providing additional practice of the skill taught in the lesson.

Homework Practice The Homework Practice worksheet provides an opportunity for additional computational practice. The Homework Practice worksheet includes word problems that address the skill taught in the lesson.

Problem-Solving Practice The Problem-Solving Practice worksheet presents additional reinforcement in solving word problems that apply both the concepts of the lesson and some review concepts.

Enrich The Enrich worksheet presents activities that extend the concepts of the lesson. Some Enrich materials are designed to widen students' perspectives on the mathematics they are learning. These worksheets are written for use with all levels of students.

Resources for Problem-Solving Strategy and Problem-Solving Investigation Lessons In recognition of the importance of problem-solving strategies, worksheets for problem-solving lessons follow a slightly different format. For problem-solving lessons, a two-page Reteach worksheet offers a complete model for choosing a problem-solving strategy. For each Problem-Solving Strategy lesson, Reteach and Homework Practice worksheets offer reinforcement of

Investigation worksheets include a model strategy on the Reteach worksheets and provide problems requiring several alternate strategies on the Homework Practice and Skills Practice worksheets.

Assessment Options The assessment masters in the *Chapter 14 Resource Masters* offer a wide variety of assessment tools for monitoring progress as well as final assessment.

Individual Progress Checklist This checklist explains the chapter's goals or objectives. Teachers can record whether a student's mastery of each objective is beginning (B), developing (D), or mastered (M). The checklist includes space to record notes to parents as well as other pertinent observations.

Chapter Diagnostic Test This one-page test assesses students' grasp of skills that are needed for success in the chapter.

Chapter Pretest This one-page quick check of the chapter's concepts is useful for determining pacing. Performance on the pretest can help you determine which concepts can be covered quickly and which specific concepts may need additional time.

Mid-Chapter Test This one-page chapter test provides an option to assess the first half of the chapter. It includes both multiple-choice and free-response questions.

Quizzes Three free-response quizzes offer quick assessment opportunities at appropriate intervals in the chapter.

Vocabulary Test This one-page test focuses on chapter vocabulary. It is suitable for all students. It includes a list of vocabulary words and questions to assess students' knowledge of the words.

Oral Assessment Although this two-page assessment is designed to be used with all students, the interview format focuses on assessing chapter content assimilated by ELL students.

Chapter Project Rubric This one-page rubric is designed for use in assessing the chapter project. You may want to distribute copies of the rubric when you assign the project and use the rubric to record each student's chapter project score.

Foldables Rubric This one-page rubric is designed to assess the Foldables graphic organizer. The rubric is written to the students, telling them what you will be looking for as you evaluate their completed Foldables graphic organizer.

Leveled Chapter Tests

- **Form 1** assesses basic chapter concepts through multiple-choice questions and is designed for use with on-level students.

- **Form 2A** is designed for on-level students and is primarily for those who may have missed the Form 1 test. It may be used as a retest for students who received additional instruction following the Form 1 test.

- **Form 2B** is designed for students with a below-level command of the English language.

- **Form 2C** is a free-response test designed for on-level students.

- **Form 2D** is written for students with a below-level command of the English language.

- **Form 3** is a free-response test written for above-level students.

- **Extended-Response Test** is an extended response test for on-level students.

Cumulative Test Practice This three-page test, aimed at on-level students, offers multiple-choice questions and free-response questions.

Student Recording Sheet This one-page recording sheet is for the standardized test in the Student Edition.

Answers

The answers for the Anticipation Guide and Lesson Resources are provided as reduced pages with answers appearing in black. Full size line-up answer keys are provided for the Assessment Masters.

Name _____ Date _____

Graphic Organizer

Use this graphic organizer to take notes on **Chapter 14: Measure Perimeter, Area, and Volume.** Fill in the missing sections of the graphic organizer.

Measurement	Formula	Example
perimeter of a square		
perimeter of a rectangle		
area of a rectangle		
area of a square		
volume of a rectangular prism		

Name _____ Date _____

Student-Built Glossary

This is an alphabetical list of new vocabulary terms you will learn in **Chapter 14: Measure Perimeter, Area, and Volume.** As you study the chapter, complete each term's definition or description. Remember to add the page number where you found the term. Add this page to your math study notebook to review vocabulary at the end of the chapter.

Vocabulary Term	Found on Page	Definition/Description/Example
area		
base		
cone		
cylinder		
edge		
face		
perimeter		

Name _____ Date _____

Student-Built Glossary (continued)

Vocabulary Term	Found on Page	Definition/Description/Example
polygon		
polyhedron		
prism		
rectangular prism		
surface area		
three-dimensional figure		
vertex		
volume		

Dear Family,

Today my class started Chapter 14: Measure Perimeter, Area, and Volume. I will be learning to find the perimeters of polygons. I will also be learning to find the areas of rectangles and triangles. And I will learn about the volume of three-dimensional figures. Here are my vocabulary words and an activity that we can do together.

Sincerely, _____

Key Vocabulary

Area: The number of square units needed to cover the inside of a region or plane figure.

Cone: A solid that has a circular base and one curved surface from the base to a vertex.

Perimeter: The distance around a shape or region.

Polygon: A closed figure made up of line segments that do not cross each other.

Prism: A polyhedron with two parallel congruent faces, called bases.

Three-dimensional figure: A solid figure.

Volume: The number of cubic units needed to fill a three-dimensional figure or solid figure.

Activity

Use construction paper to cut out 4 rectangles of different sizes. Use a ruler to measure the length and width in centimeters. Label each rectangle with its corresponding height and width. Find the area and perimeter of each rectangle.

Books to Read

Pigs Will Be Pigs
by Amy Axelrod

Mr. Archimedes' Bath
by Pamela Allen

The Tangram Magician
by Ernst & Ernst

Estimada familia:

Hoy mi clase comenzó el **Capítulo 14: Mide el perímetro, el área y el volumen.** Aprenderé a calcular los perímetros de polígonos. También aprenderé a calcular las áreas de rectángulos y de triángulos. Y aprenderé además sobre el volumen de figuras tridimensionales. A continuación, están mis palabras del vocabulario y una actividad que podemos realizar juntos.

Sinceramente, _____

Vocabulario clave

Área: Número de unidades cuadradas necesarias para cubrir el interior de una región o figura plana.

Cono: Sólido que tiene una base circular y una superficie curva desde la base hasta un vértice.

Perímetro: Distancia alrededor de una figura o región.

Prisma coliedro: con dos caras paralelas y congruentes, llamadas bases.

Polumen: Número de unidades cúbicas necesarias para llenar una figura tridimensional o sólida.

Figura tridimensional: Figura sólida.

Polígono: Figura cerrada compuesta por segmentos de recta que no se intersecan.

Actividad

Usen cartulina para recortar 4 rectángulos de diferentes tamaños. Utilicen una regla para medir la longitud y el ancho en centímetros. Rotulen cada rectángulo con su altura y ancho correspondientes. Calculen el área y el perímetro de cada rectángulo.

Libros recomendados

Pigs Will Be Pigs
(Los cerdos seguirán siendo cerdos)
de Amy Axelrod

Mr. Archimedes' Bath
(El baño del Sr. Arquímedes)
de Pamela Allen

The Tangram Magician
(El mago del tangram)
de Ernst & Ernst

Name _____ Date _____

Anticipation Guide

Measure Perimeter, Area, and Volume

STEP 1 | *Before you begin Chapter 14*

- Read each statement.
- Decide whether you agree (A) or disagree (D) with the statement.
- Write A or D in the first column OR if you are not sure whether you agree or disagree, write NS (not sure).

STEP 1 A, D, or NS	Statement	STEP 2 A or D
	1. A three-dimensional figure is a solid.	
	2. Volume is the number of cubic units needed to fill a three-dimensional figure or solid figure.	
	3. Area is the number of square units needed to cover the inside of a region or plane figure.	
	4. Perimeter is the distance across a shape or a region.	
	5. Perimeter and volume are the same measure.	
	6. A triangular prism has triangular bases.	

STEP 2 | *After you complete Chapter 14*

- Reread each statement and complete the last column by entering an A (agree) or a D (disagree).
- Did any of your opinions about the statements change from the first column?
- For those statements that you mark with a D, use a separate sheet of paper to explain why you disagree. Use examples, if possible.

Name _____ Date _____

Game

Pentomino Madness

Ready

- 5 index cards
- Scissors
- Ruler

Set

Use the ruler to help you cut the index cards into squares of exactly the same size. A pentomino is a figure that has an area of exactly 5 unit squares where each square is connected on at least one full side to another square.

GO!

1. Have player 1 arrange the set of squares into a different pentomino than the one shown at the right.

2. Determine the perimeter of the pentomino by counting the outside edges. Player 1 receives this number of points.

3. Have player 2 arrange the set of squares into a different pentomino.

4. Determine the perimeter of the pentomino. Player 2 receives this number of points.

5. Have the players continue taking turns for 5 rounds. A round consists of both player 1 and player 2 creating a pentomino.

6. Add up the points. The player with the most points at the end of the 5 rounds is the winner.

Name _____ Date _____

Reteach

Perimeters of Polygons

Perimeter is the distance around a closed figure.

To find the perimeter of a figure, add the lengths of all the sides.

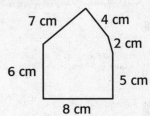

$P = 6 \text{ cm} + 7 \text{ cm} + 4 \text{ cm} + 2 \text{ cm} + 5 \text{ cm} + 8 \text{ cm}$
$P = 32 \text{ cm}$

Find the perimeter of each figure.

1.

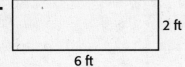

6 ft
2 ft

_____

2.

7 cm
3 cm

_____

3.

60 mm
20 mm

_____

4.

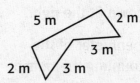

5 m   2 m
3 m
2 m   3 m

_____

5.

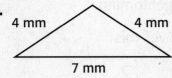

4 mm   4 mm
7 mm

_____

6.

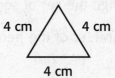

4 cm   4 cm
4 cm

_____

7.

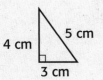

5 cm
4 cm
3 cm

_____

8.

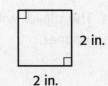

2 in.
2 in.

_____

Name _____ Date _____

Skills Practice

Perimeters of Polygons

Find the perimeter of each figure.

1.

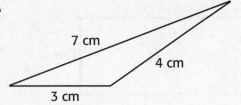

2.

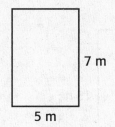

_____

_____

3.

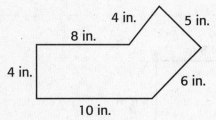

4.

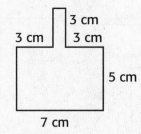

_____

_____

5.

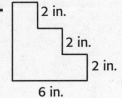

6.

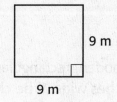

_____

_____

Solve.

7. Find the perimeter of an isosceles triangle whose sides are 8 inches and whose base is 4 inches.

_____

8. Molly has 60 feet of fencing to go around the perimeter of her garden. She wants the garden to be a square. How long should each side be?

_____

Name _____ Date _____

Homework Practice

Perimeters of Polygons

Find the perimeter of each square or rectangle.

1.   13 ft

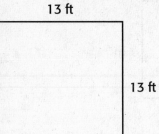
13 ft

_____

2.   4.76 m

1.93 m

_____

3.   11 ft

$2\frac{1}{2}$ ft

_____

4.   4.8 m

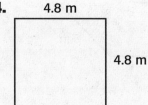
4.8 m

_____

5. Neil made a wooden, rectangular picture frame that is 14 inches long and 10 inches wide. If he charges $2.50 per foot, how much will he sell this frame for?

_____

Spiral Review

(Lesson 13–9)

6. Create a pattern using transformations.

_____

10

Name _____ Date _____

Problem-Solving Practice

Perimeters of Polygons

Solve.

1. Hannah wants to create a fenced enclosure for her dog. To figure out how much fencing she needs, Hannah made a drawing of the enclosure.

   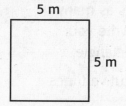

   How much fencing will she need?

   _____

2. Johanna has a garden that is in the shape of a regular pentagon. Each side of the pentagon is 7 ft long. She decides to place a small, decorative wood fence around the perimeter. The fencing is sold in boxes of 5 pieces. Each piece has a length of 18 in. How many boxes of fencing will Johanna need to buy?

   _____

3. A rectangular driveway is 40 ft long and 14 ft wide. What is the perimeter of the driveway?

   _____

4. Tara has a rectangular garden that is 10 ft long and 4 ft wide. She wants to put a small fence around it. If fencing costs $1.50 per ft, how much will the fence cost?

   _____

5. Vincent is designing a rectangular garden. The outside of the garden will measure 12 ft long and 5 ft wide. He plans to use tiles around the inside edge of the border. The tiles are squares, and each side measures 1 ft. After placing the tiles, Vincent will put a small fence around the inside, against the tiles. How many feet of fencing does he need?

   _____

Name _____ Date _____

Enrich

Perimeter of Rectangles

Play this game with a partner. Take turns.

How to Play

- Toss two 1–6 number cubes. Use the two numbers rolled to form a 2-digit number.

- If possible, draw a rectangle on the grid below that has as many units in its perimeter as the two-digit number rolled. Write your initials in it. Your rectangle may not overlap another rectangle.

- When the number cubes have been rolled four consecutive times without a rectangle being drawn, the game is over.

The player who draws more rectangles wins.

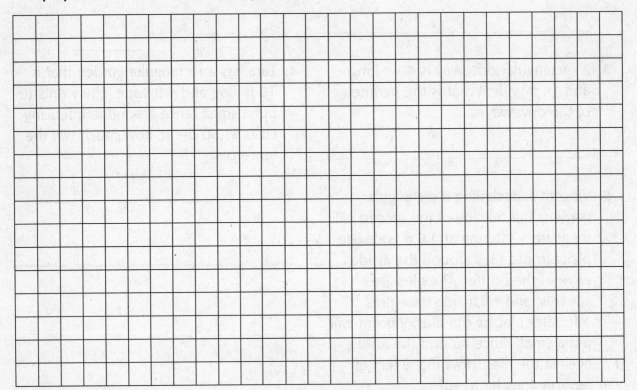

Describe a strategy you and your partner used to play this game.

_____

_____

Name _____ Date _____

Reteach

Area

Area is the number of square units that cover the surface of a closed figure. One way to find the area of a figure is to use grid paper and count the number of square units.

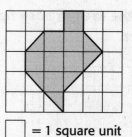

☐ = 1 square unit

There are 7 whole squares and 6 half squares.

The 6 half squares equal 3 whole squares.

The area of the figure is 10 square units.

When you cannot count square units or half square units exactly, you can estimate the area.

Step 1 Count the whole squares. There are 20 whole squares.

Step 2 Count the squares that are partly covered and divide that number by 2.

$8 \div 2 = 4$

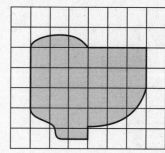

Step 3 Add the numbers from Step 1 and Step 2.

$20 + 4 = 24$

The area of the figure is 24 square units.

Estimate the area of each figure. Each square represents 1 square centimeter.

1.

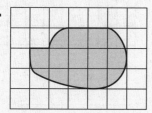

$A =$ _____ square centimeters

2.

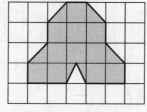

$A =$ _____ square centimeters

3.

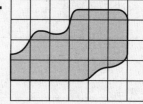

$A =$ _____ square centimeters

13

Name _____ Date _____

Skills Practice

Area

Estimate the area of each figure. Each square represents 1 square centimeter.

1.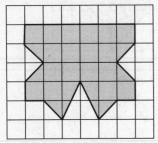

A = _____

2.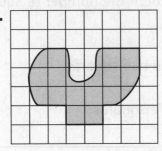

A = _____

3.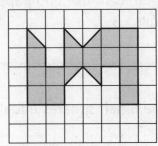

A = _____

4.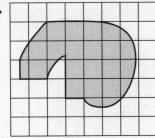

A = _____

5.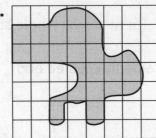

A = _____

6.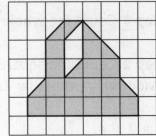

A = _____

7.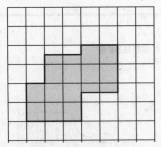

A = _____

8.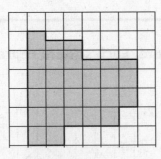

A = _____

9.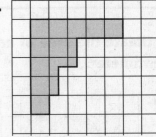

A = _____

Name _____ Date _____

Homework Practice

Area

Estimate the area of each figure. Each square represents 1 square centimeter.

1.
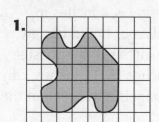

_____

2.
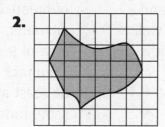

_____

3.
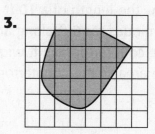

_____

4.
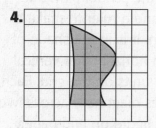

_____

5.
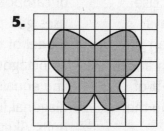

_____

6.
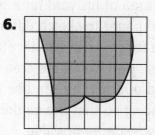

_____

Spiral Review

Find the perimeter of each square or rectangle.   (Lesson 14–1)

7.
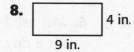
3 m

3 m

_____

8.
4 in.

9 in.

_____

9.
3 yd

7 yd

_____

Name _____ Date _____

Problem-Solving Practice

Area

Solve. Use grid paper.

1. Dan has a kitchen countertop that runs the length of a 10-ft room and continues for 6 ft along another wall. The countertop is 2 ft wide. What is the area of the countertop?

2. Denzel is toasting 4 bagels and 2 slices of bread. Each bagel is 4 inches in diameter. Each slice of bread has an area of 9 square inches. If the toaster oven rack is 8 inches by 11 inches, can he toast all the bagels and bread at the same time?

3. Pablo has 64 ft of fencing to enclose an area of his yard for a garden. Use grid paper to sketch different ways the fencing can exactly enclose an area. Determine the area of each and find out how he can use the 64 ft of fencing so that the garden will be the greatest area possible.

4. Regina needs to make a stop sign out of cardboard for the school play. She uses grid paper and a ruler to make a model of the sign. It is in the shape of an octagon. Each horizontal or vertical line equals three units on the grid. Each diagonal line goes diagonally across two units. Sketch the figure on grid paper. How many squares on the grid are included in the sign? _____ squares

   If each unit on the grid equals 4 in., how many square inches of cardboard will Regina need for the sign?

5. Mabel was helping her mother tile the kitchen floor. The size of the kitchen is 7 feet by 12 feet. The counters are 2 feet deep and run along the floor of one of the shorter walls. The refrigerator takes up another 6 square feet of floor space. If each tile is a 6-inch square, how many tiles are needed for the kitchen floor?

6. Mai used grid paper to draw plans for a dog pen. She connected the following points in order: (1, 0), (1, 5), (4, 5), (4, 2), (6, 2), (6, 0), and (1, 0). The side of each square on the grid paper represents 2 ft of the dog pen. If Steve is covering the ground in Mai's dog pen with straw, how many square feet will he need to cover?

Name _____ Date _____

Enrich

Perimeter and Area of Irregular Figures

You are a landscape designer. Your most recent project is a yard that measures 40 meters by 50 meters. You will include the features below.

- an irregularly-shaped pond that is between 100 and 200 square meters
- an irregularly-shaped vegetable garden that is between 50 and 100 square meters
- an irregularly-shaped flower garden that is between 50 and 100 square meters
- fences for the gardens
- a patio that is between 200 and 300 square meters.

Sketch your design on the grid below. Include a scale that explains what each square represents.

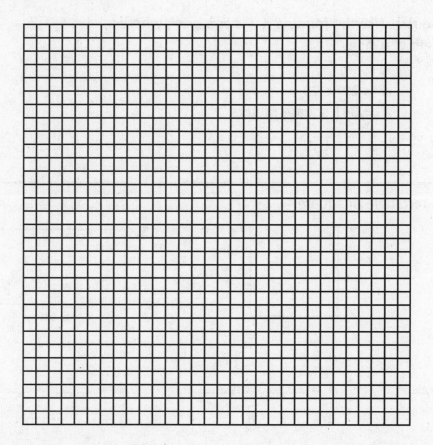

How many feet of fencing do you need for the gardens? Explain how you found your answers.

_____

_____

_____

Name _____ Date _____

Reteach

Areas of Rectangles and Squares

Area is the number of square units needed to cover a figure. To find the area of a rectangle or square, you can multiply its length times its width. This can be shown by a formula.

Find the area of the rectangle. Use the formula $A = \ell w$, where A = area, ℓ = length, and w = width.

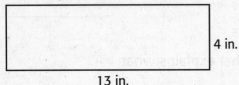

4 in.

13 in.

$A = \ell w$
$A = 13 \times 4$
$A = 52$ square inches

Find the area of the square. Use the formula $A = s \times s$ or s^2, where A = area and s = length of a side.

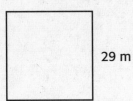

29 m

29 m

$A = s^2$
$A = 29 \times 29$
$A = 841$ square meters

Find the area of each rectangle or square.

1.

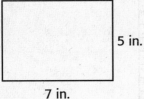

5 in.

7 in.

$A = \ell w$

$A =$ _____ × _____

$A =$ _____ in.²

2.

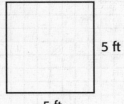

5 ft

5 ft

$A = s^2$

$A =$ _____ × _____

$A =$ _____ ft²

3.

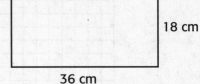

18 cm

36 cm

$A = \ell w$

$A =$ _____ × _____

$A =$ _____ cm²

4.

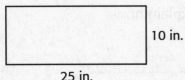

10 in.

25 in.

$A =$ _____

5.

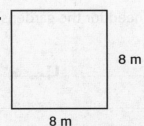

8 m

8 m

$A =$ _____

6.

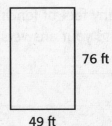

76 ft

49 ft

$A =$ _____

Name _____ Date _____

Skills Practice

Areas of Rectangles

Find the area of each rectangle or square.

1.
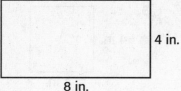
4 in.
8 in.

A = _____

2.
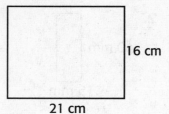
16 cm
21 cm

A = _____

3.
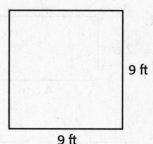
9 ft
9 ft

A = _____

4.
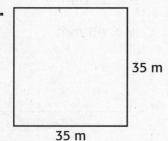
35 m
35 m

A = _____

5.
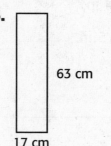
63 cm
17 cm

A = _____

6.
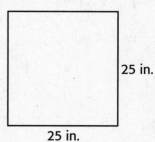
25 in.
25 in.

A = _____

Find each missing measurement.

7.

z
12 cm

A = 48 square centimeters

z = _____

8.
b
b

A = 16 square feet

b = _____

9.
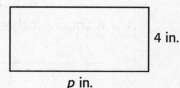
4 in.
p in.

A = 72 square inches

p = _____

Solve.

10. A family room is 24 feet long and 18 feet wide. What is the area of the family room?

_____

11. A square carpet is 36 meters on each side. What area will the carpet cover?

_____

Name _____ Date _____

Homework Practice

Areas of Rectangles

Find the area of each rectangle.

1.

2 cm

4 cm

_____

2.

40 mm

15 mm

_____

3.

4 in.

4 in.

_____

4. rectangle

$\ell = 3$ yd

$w = 4$ yd

_____

5. rectangle

$\ell = 4$ in.

$W = 5$ in.

_____

6. rectangle

$\ell = 32$ mm

$w = 46$ mm

_____

Find the unknown width.

7. rectangle

$\ell = 3$ in.

$A = 6$ square inches

$w =$ _____

8. rectangle

$\ell = 45$ mm

$A = 3{,}150$ square millimeters

$w =$ _____

Spiral Review

Solve.

9. Mike's room is 12 feet by 15 feet. How many square feet of carpeting does he need to cover the entire floor?

_____

10. Helen is planting tomatoes in her garden. She can place 3 plants per square foot. How many plants does she need if her garden measures 7 ft by 6 ft?

_____

14-3

Problem-Solving Practice

Areas of Rectangles

Solve.

1. Felicia wants to clean the rug in her room. She buys carpet cleaner that will clean 40 ft². Find the area of her rug. Will she have enough carpet cleaner?

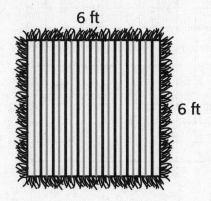

6 ft

6 ft

_____

2. Lori wants to buy a flower mat that has seeds and fertilizer in it for her garden. She made a diagram of her garden. What is the area of the flower mat that she needs?

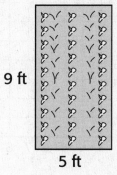

9 ft

5 ft

_____

3. The playing area of a college's football field measures 100 yd by 53 yd wide. How much area does the football team have to play on?

_____

4. Mr. and Mrs. Wilkes want to make a patio in their yard. The patio will be 15 ft long and 10 ft wide. Each patio stone covers 1 square ft and costs $2. How much will they spend on patio tiles?

_____

5. You have 100 ft of fencing to make a pen for your dog. You want your dog to have the biggest play area possible. What shape would you make the pen?

_____

6. The Carsons are putting a rectangular swimming pool in their backyard. The pool will measure 20 ft by 12 ft. They plan to have a cement walkway around the pool, which should measure 4 ft wide. What is the area of the walkway?

_____

Name _____ Date _____

Enrich

Areas of Polygons

Graph the ordered pairs. Connect the points.
Record the length, width, and area of the rectangle.

1. (2, 3), (2, 7), (9, 3), (9, 7)

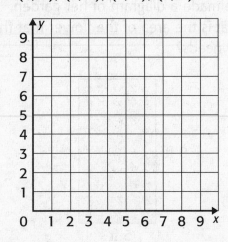

$\ell =$ _____ $w =$ _____ $A =$ _____

2. (2, 1), (2, 8), (7, 1), (7, 8)

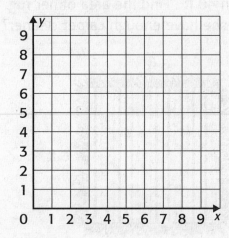

$\ell =$ _____ $w =$ _____ $A =$ _____

3. (6, 1), (6, 6), (1, 1), (1, 6)

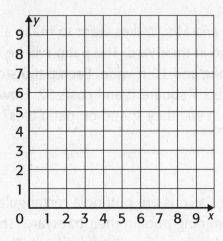

$\ell =$ _____ $w =$ _____ $A =$ _____

4. (9, 8), (9, 1), (1, 1), (1, 8)

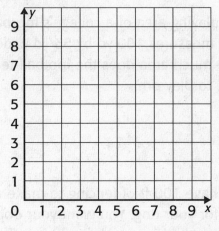

$\ell =$ _____ $w =$ _____ $A =$ _____

Compare the length and width of each rectangle to the coordinates you graphed.

_____

_____

_____

14-4

Reteach

Geometry: Three-Dimensional Figures

Prisms are three-dimensional figures. Their parts have special names.

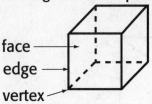

face
edge
vertex

Face: flat surface on a prism or pyramid
Edge: segment where 2 faces meet
Vertex: point where edges meet
Prisms can be named by the shape of their bases.

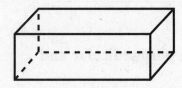

6 faces
12 edges
8 vertices
The bases are rectangular.
This prism is a rectangular prism.

Describe parts of each figure that are parallel and congruent. Then identify the figure.

1.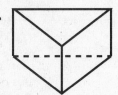

    _____

    _____

2.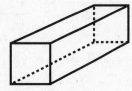

    _____

    _____

3. 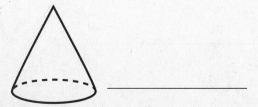 _____

4.

23

14-4

Skills Practice

Geometry: Three-Dimensional Figures

Describe parts of each figure that are parallel and congruent. Then identify the figure.

1.

2.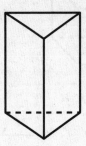

3.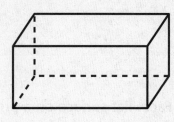

_____

_____

_____

Describe parts of each figure that are perpendicular and congruent. Then identify the figure.

4.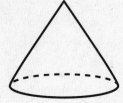

5.

6.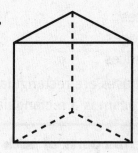

_____

_____

_____

Solve.

7. Describe the number of faces, vertices and edges in a can of soup. Identify the shape of the can.

_____

Name _____ Date _____

Homework Practice

Geometry: Three-Dimensional Figures

Describe parts of each figure that are perpendicular and congruent. Then identify the figure.

1.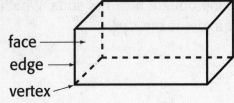

face →
edge →
vertex →

_____

_____

2.

_____

_____

3.

_____

_____

Spiral Review

Find the area of each rectangle.   (Lesson 14–3)

4.
4 in.
13 in.

5.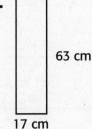
63 cm
17 cm

_____

6.
29 m
29 m

_____

25

14-4

Problem-Solving Practice

Geometry: Three-Dimensional Figures

Solve.

1. Ricardo made a simple drawing of his house. It is a polyhedron with 6 faces. Four faces are rectangular, and 2 are square. What kind of figure is it?

   _____

2. Diane bought a can of soda. What kind of figure is the can?

   _____

3. Gary is playing a board game. When it is his turn, he tosses a kind of polyhedron that is used in many board games. What kind of polyhedron is it?

   _____

   How many faces, edges, and vertices does it have?

   _____

4. When Ben bought a poster, the salesperson placed it in a tube to protect it. What kind of shape is the tube?

   _____

   If the tube is slit down its side and laid flat, what shape would it make?

   _____

5. Describe the shape of a rectangular pyramid. How does it compare to a triangular prism?

   _____

   _____

   _____

6. What kind of shape is a funnel? Describe the number of faces and vertices it has.

   _____

   _____

   _____

Name _____ Date _____

Enrich

Three-Dimensional Figures

Complete the table for these three-dimensional shapes.

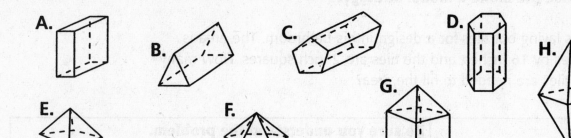

A. B. C. D. H.

E. F. G.

Figure	Number of Faces	Number of Vertices	Total Faces and Vertices	Number of Edges
A				
B				
C				
D				
E				
F				
G				
H				

Look for a pattern in the table above. Then complete this statement.

The sum of the number of faces and vertices is equal to the number of

_____ plus _____ .

Let f = number of faces, v = number of vertices, and e = number of edges.
Write the statement you completed above as an equation.

_____

Write a formula for the number of edges.

_____

14–5

Reteach

Problem-Solving Strategy

Make a Model

Solve. Use the *make a model* strategy.

Pedro is laying out tiles for a design in his bathroom. The area is
20 inches by 16 inches, and the tiles are 2 inch squares. How many
square tiles are needed to fill the area?

Step 1 Understand	**Be sure you understand the problem.** Pedro is laying 2-inch tile in a 20-inch by 16-inch area.
Step 2 Plan Make a model using paper to find the number of tiles needed.	**Make a plan.** You can use a piece of construction paper and small square pieces of paper to represent the tiles.
Step 3 Solve	**Carry out your plan.** Make a model of the area by measuring out a 20″ × 16″ rectangle on construction paper. 20 in. 16 in. Cut out 2-inch squares from another piece of paper. Cover the 20″ × 16″ area completely with the squares. It will take 80 squares or tiles.
Step 4 Check	**Is the solution reasonable?** Reread the problem. Calculate to check your answer. Find the area of 20″ × 16″. It is 320 square inches. Each 2 inch tile has an area of 2″ × 2″ = 4 square inches. 320 square inches ÷ 4 square inches = 80 tiles

Name _____ Date _____

Reteaching

Problem-Solving Strategy (continued)

Solve. Use the *make a model* strategy.

1. Hugo is making a block tower. Each block is a 4-inch square and is 1 inch thick. If he has 35 blocks, what is the tallest height he can make with the blocks?

   _____

2. Susan wants to organize her bookshelf in her bedroom. It measures 36 inches long, and there are three shelves. If she has 25 two-inch wide books, 15 three-inch wide books, and 32 one-inch wide books, will she be able to fit them on the three shelves? If not, how many of each book will not fit?

   _____

   _____

3. Patricia is making a clay game board. Each square needs to be 2 inches. If the board will be 16 inches square, how many total squares will it have?

   _____

4. Pablo has a sheet of stickers that is 11 inches long. Each sticker is a 1 inch circle and there are 10 in each row. How many stickers are there on one page?

   _____

5. Charo is making a picture frame with shells she found. Each shell is 2 inches long. If she makes a rectangular frame out of 20 shells, how large can she make the frame?

   _____

29

Name _____ Date _____

Skills Practice

Problem-Solving Strategy

Solve. Use the *make a model* strategy.

1. Ping and Kuri are designing a small end table using 1-inch tiles. If Kuri picks three times as many tiles out than Ping, and Ping picks out 24 tiles, how many total tiles are there? The area of the table is 19 inches by 5 inches. Will they have enough tiles to cover the tabletop?

   _____

2. The Miller family is redoing their garden. If they have a garden that is 500 square feet, and one side is 10 feet long, what is the length of the other side of the garden? If they plant 5 trees that need to be 5 feet apart and 5 feet away from the fence around the garden, will they have the space?

   _____

3. Bob is organizing his pantry. If he has cracker boxes that measure 12 inches high, 2 inches wide, and 10 inches long, how many boxes can he fit on a 24-inch-long shelf that is 14 inches deep?

   _____

4. You are packing picnic baskets for a day camp. Each basket needs to carry 8 square sandwiches, 8 apples, and 8 juice boxes. Would the best basket be an 18″ × 15″ × 9″ basket, a 72″ × 40″ × 18″ basket, or a 12″ × 6″ × 8″ basket?

   _____

5. Roberto wants to build a long train track. If each piece of track is 6 inches long, and he has 42 pieces, can he make a track that is 20 feet long? Can he make a track that is 22 feet long?

   _____

Name _____ Date _____

Homework Practice

Problem-Solving Strategy

Solve. Use the *make a model* strategy.

1. Nan and Sato are designing a coffee table using 4 inch tiles. Nan uses 30 tiles and Sato uses half as many. How many total tiles did they use? If the area of the table is 36 inches by 24 inches, will they have enough tiles for the table? If not, how many more will they need?

   _____

2. The Jones family is landscaping their yard. If they have a yard that is 160 square feet, and one side is 10 feet long, what is the length of the other side of the garden? If they plant 3 bushes that need to be 3 feet apart and 3 feet away from the fence around the yard, will they have the space?

   _____

3. Bob is organizing his closet. If he has clothing bins that measure 20 inches high, 18 inches wide, and 14 inches long, how many bins can he fit in a 60-inch long closet that is 30 inches deep and 72 inches high?

   _____

4. Roberto wants to build a brick wall. Each brick layer is 3 inches thick, and the wall will be 18 inches tall. How many layers will it have?

   _____

Spiral Review

Identify each figure.   (Lesson 14–4)

5. This polyhedron has six rectangular faces. _____

6. This prism has triangular bases. _____

7. This is a solid that has a circular base and one curved surface from the base to a vertex. _____

31

14–5

Enrich

Follow Directions

Follow the directions to solve the problem. You may use cubes.

The rectangular prism to the right is made of 1-inch cubes. The prism is 2 inches wide by 4 inches long by 3 inches high.

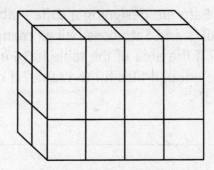

1. What is the total surface area of the prism?

   _____

2. Label the front layer of cubes. Use the capital letters *A* through *D* to label the cubes in the first row, *E* through *H* to label the cubes in the second row, and *I* through *L* to label the cubes in the third row. Then draw a diagram that would show what the figure would look like if you removed cube *D*. How would the surface area of the cube change if you removed cube *D*?

   _____

   _____

3. Draw a model that shows what the figure would look like if you removed cube *C*. How would the surface area of the cube change if you removed cube *C*?

   _____

   _____

   _____

4. Name a cube that could be removed to give a surface area of 56 square inches.

   _____

   _____

5. Cube *a* is behind cube *A*, cube *b* is behind cube *B*, cube *d* is behind cube *D*, and so on. Name a pair of cubes that could be removed to give a surface area of 50 square inches.

   _____

   _____

Name _____ Date _____

Reteach

Volume of Prisms

Volume is the amount of space a three-dimensional figure encloses. To find the volume of a rectangular prism, you can use a formula.

Find the volume of the rectangular prism. Use the formula $V = \ell wh$, where V = volume, ℓ = length, w = width, and h = height.

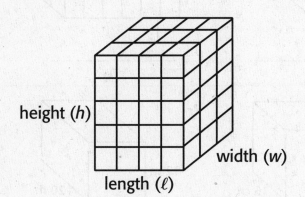

height (*h*)

width (*w*)

length (*ℓ*)

$V = \ell wh$
$V = 4 \times 3 \times 5$
$V = 60$ cubic units

Find the volume of each prism.

1.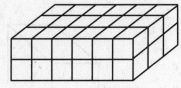

$\ell =$ _____ units

$w =$ _____ units

$h =$ _____ units

$V = \ell wh$

$V =$ ____ $\times$ ____ $\times$ ____

$V =$ _____ cubic units

2.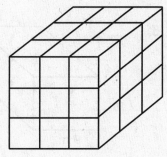

$\ell =$ _____ units

$w =$ _____ units

$h =$ _____ units

$V = \ell wh$

$V =$ ____ $\times$ ____ $\times$ ____

$V =$ _____ cubic units

3.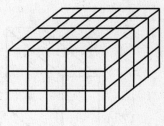

$\ell =$ _____ units

$w =$ _____ units

$h =$ _____ units

$V = \ell wh$

$V =$ ____ $\times$ ____ $\times$ ____

$V =$ _____ cubic units

Name _____ Date _____

Skills Practice

Volume of Prisms

Find the volume of each prism.

1.
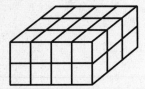

V = _____

2.
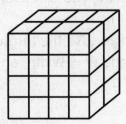

V = _____

3.
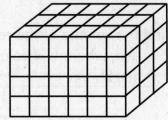

V = _____

4.
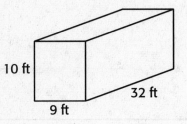
10 ft
9 ft
32 ft

V = _____

5.
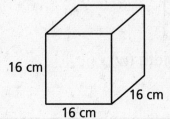
16 cm
16 cm
16 cm

V = _____

6.
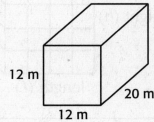
12 m
12 m
20 m

V = _____

7.
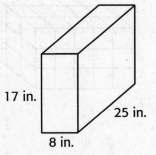
17 in.
8 in.
25 in.

V = _____

8.
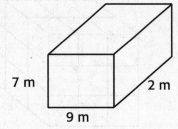
7 m
9 m
2 m

V = _____

9.
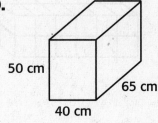
50 cm
40 cm
65 cm

V = _____

Solve.

10. The dimensions of a gift box for jewelry are 6 inches by 3 inches by 2 inches. What is the volume of the gift box?

_____

11. The dimensions of a shoe box are 13 inches by 9 inches by 4 inches. What is the volume of the shoe box?

_____

Name _____ Date _____

Homework Practice

Volume of Prisms

Find the volume of each prism.

1.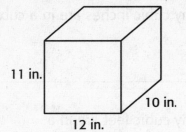
11 in.
12 in.
10 in.

_____

2.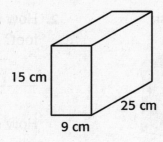
15 cm
9 cm
25 cm

_____

3.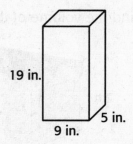
19 in.
9 in.
5 in.

_____

4. What is the volume of a rectangular box that has a base of 50 square inches and a height of 12 inches?

_____

5. Bernice made a rectangular wooden tool box that has a base of 50 square centimeters and a height of 35 cm. What is the volume?

_____

Spiral Review

Use any strategy to solve. (Lesson 15–5)

6. Ali has a loaf of bread that he needs to slice for his family's dinner. How many cuts does he need to make if he needs 6 equal-size slices of bread?

_____

7. Maggie's older sister is repaying her student loans. Her loans, including interest, total $9,985. How much are her monthly payments if she plans to repay the loans in 8 years?

_____

Name _____ Date _____

Problem-Solving Practice

Volume of Prisms

Solve.

1. Find the volume of the chest.

   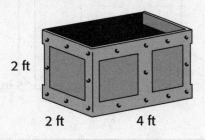

   2 ft

   2 ft   4 ft

   _____

2. How many cubic inches are in a cubic foot?

   _____

   How many cubic feet are in a cubic yard?

   _____

3. The Donaldson's swimming pool measures 15 m long, 8 m wide, and 3 m deep. How many cubic meters of water will the pool hold?

   _____

4. Myra is baking a cake in a pan that measures 9 in. by 13 in. by 2 in. How many cubic inches of cake will the pan hold?

   _____

5. To save money, a local shipping company wants to purchase packing peanuts in bulk. The plant manager built a storage container that is 4 yds long, 10 yds wide, and 2 yds tall to store the peanuts. If the manager purchases bags that contain 7 ft³ of peanuts, how many bags of peanuts will it take to fill the container?

   _____

6. Paul is shopping for a refrigerator. He needs to compare the sizes and volumes to decide which refrigerator to buy. He needs a refrigerator with the dimensions shown below in order to fit in his kitchen. Find the volume of the refrigerator.

   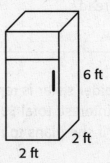

   6 ft

   2 ft

   2 ft

   _____

Name _____ Date _____

Enrich

Volume of Rectangular Prism

Rectangular prisms of different shapes can have the same volume. These rectangular prisms have different shapes, but the volume of both prisms is 24 cm³.

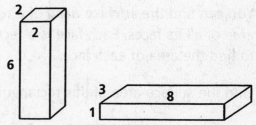

The table below shows the volumes of different rectangular prisms. For each volume, write as many different sets of three numbers that could represent a rectangular prism with that volume. One has been started for you.

32 in³	40 m³	60 cm³	72 mm³
1, 1, 32			

What strategy did you use to complete the table?

_____

_____

_____

_____

_____

_____

Name _____ Date _____

Reteach

Surface Areas of Prisms

You can find the **surface area** of a rectangular prism by finding the total area of all its faces. Each face is a rectangle, so use the formula $A = lw$ to find the area of each face.

Find the surface area of this rectangular prism.

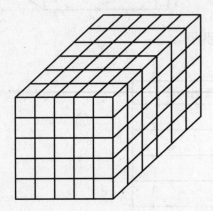

Front face:	$5 \times 5 = 25$ square units
Back face:	$5 \times 5 = 25$ square units
Top face:	$5 \times 6 = 30$ square units
Bottom face:	$5 \times 6 = 30$ square units
Right face:	$5 \times 6 = 30$ square units
Left face:	$5 \times 6 = 30$ square units
Total surface area:	170 square units

Find the surface area of each rectangular prism.

1.

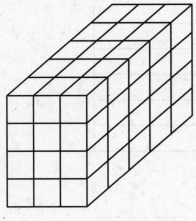

Front face: _____ × _____ = _____ square units

Back face: _____ × _____ = _____ square units

Top face: _____ × _____ = _____ square units

Bottom face: _____ × _____ = _____ square units

Right face: _____ × _____ = _____ square units

Left face: _____ × _____ = _____ square units

Total surface area: _____ square units

2.

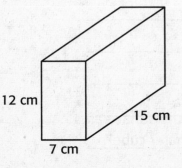

12 cm 15 cm 7 cm

Front face: _____ × _____ = _____ cm²

Back face: _____ × _____ = _____ cm²

Top face: _____ × _____ = _____ cm²

Bottom face: _____ × _____ = _____ cm²

Right face: _____ × _____ = _____ cm²

Left face: _____ × _____ = _____ cm²

Total surface area: _____ cm²

Name _____ Date _____

Skills Practice

Surface Areas of Prisms

Find the surface area of each rectangular prism.

1.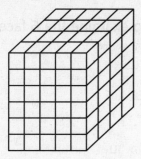

2.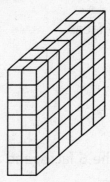

_____ _____

3.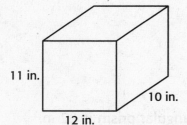

11 in. 12 in. 10 in.

4.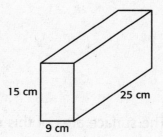

15 cm 9 cm 25 cm

5.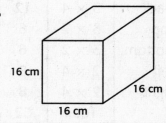

16 cm 16 cm 16 cm

_____ _____ _____

6.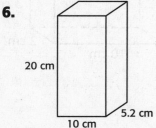

20 cm 10 cm 5.2 cm

7.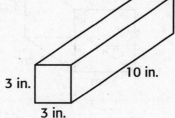

3 in. 3 in. 10 in.

8.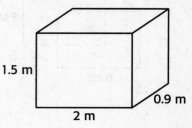

1.5 m 2 m 0.9 m

_____ _____ _____

Problem Solving
Solve.

9. What is the surface area of a cardboard shipping box that is 26 inches long, 26 inches wide, and 18 inches high?

_____

10. What is the surface area of a 9-centimeter cube?

_____

Name _____ Date _____

Homework Practice

Surface Areas of Prisms

The **surface srea** (SA) of a 3-dimensional figure is the sum of the area of all its faces.

A rectangular prism has 6 faces.

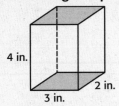

Unfold the prism to examine the 6 faces.

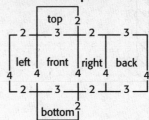

Find the area of each of the 6 faces, and add.

Face	Area	In.²
front	3 × 4	12
back	3 × 4	12
top	3 × 2	6
bottom	3 × 2	6
left	2 × 4	8
right	2 × 4	8
	Total	52

The surface area of this rectangular prism is 52 in.²

Find the surface area of each figure.

1.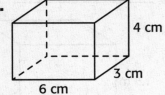

2.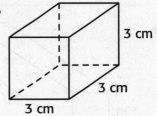

3.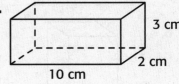

_____ _____ _____

Spiral Review

Find the volume of each prism. (Lesson 14–6)

4.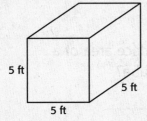

5.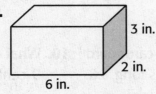

6.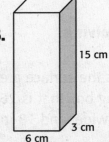

_____ _____ _____

Name _____ Date _____

Problem-Solving Practice

Surface Areas of Prisms

Solve.

1. Dylan has a toy box he wants to paint. He needs to find the surface area of the box in order to determine how much paint to buy. What is the surface area of the toy box?

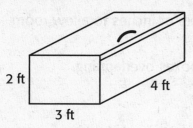

2 ft
4 ft
3 ft

_____

2. Jose is moving to a new house and has several packing boxes that are 2 ft by 2 ft by 3 ft. What is the surface area of each box?

_____

3. Julia has a music box that she wants to cover with fabric. How many square inches of fabric will she need to cover the music box?

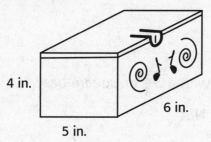

4 in.
6 in.
5 in.

_____

4. Lenny builds kitchen cabinets that measure 3 ft tall, 1.5 ft long, and 2 ft deep. What is the surface area of each cabinet?

_____

5. Lenny installs one of his cabinets from Problem 4 in a corner, attached to the ceiling. What is the surface area of the exposed faces?

_____

6. Lenny installs two of his cabinets, side-by-side on a wall, attached to the ceiling. What is the surface area of the exposed faces?

_____

41

Name _____ Date _____

Enrich

Surface Areas of Prisms

Suppose that your job is to design boxes for a gift manufacturer. You know the name of an item and its dimensions. Your job is to draw a box to fit the item. Then you have to draw its corresponding net. You need to label the dimensions on the box and net and tell the surface area of the box. When designing a box, you also need to follow these guidelines:

- Boxes must be rectangular prisms.
- Boxes should be as small as possible.
- The dimensions of each box must be in whole numbers of inches to allow room for packing materials.
- You do not have to be concerned about sides of the boxes overlapping.

Design a box for each item.

Item 1: A pottery giraffe that is $11\frac{1}{2}$ in. tall, $5\frac{1}{4}$ in. long, and $2\frac{5}{8}$ in. wide

   Box   **Net**

Surface area: _____

Item 2: A pyramid-shaped paperweight $4\frac{5}{8}$ in. tall with a $3\frac{3}{4}$ in. square base

   Box   **Net**

Surface area: _____

Name _____ Date _____

Reteach

Select Appropriate Measurement Formulas

Mr. Gonzalez wants to enclose a field for his horse. The field is 20 feet wide and 40 feet long. How much fencing will Mr. Gonzalez need? Should he find the perimeter or area of the field? Solve the problem.

The field is 20 feet by 40 feet.
You need to find how much fencing is needed.

Draw a diagram of the field. Label the length of each side.

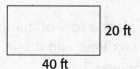

20 ft

40 ft

Think: **Perimeter** is the distance around a closed figure. $P = 2\ell + 2w$
Area is the number of square units inside a closed figure. $A = \ell w$
Volume is the space enclosed by a figure. $V = \ell wh$

You need to find the **perimeter**, or the distance around the field.
Perimeter = 2 × (length + width) = 2 × (40 + 20)

Mr. Gonzalez needs 120 feet of fencing.

Determine whether you need to find the perimeter, area, or volume. Then solve.

1. A rectangular banner is 4 feet wide and 8 feet long. How much ribbon is needed to trim the borders of the banner?

_____

2. The floor of a room needs new carpet. The room is 10 feet wide and 12 feet long. How much carpet is needed to cover the floor?

_____

Name _____ Date _____

Skills Practice

Select Appropriate Measurement Formulas

Determine whether you need to find the perimeter, area, or volume. Then solve.

1. Hayden wants to make a rectangular herb garden that is 4 feet long and 3 feet wide. She wants to plant lavender in half of the garden. How much of the garden will be covered with lavender?

   _____

2. Daniel wants to plant a row of marigolds along the border of his vegetable garden. The garden is 6 feet long and 4 feet wide. How much of the garden will need to be covered with marigolds?

   _____

3. Ms. Carmichael is building a deck with two levels. The lower level is a square. The length of each side is 5 feet. The upper level is rectangular in shape, 12 feet long and 8 feet wide. How much wood will she need to construct each level?

   _____

   _____

   _____

4. Ms. Carmichael wants to use the space underneath the lower level as storage space. If the lower level of the deck is 4 feet high off the ground, how much storage space will she have?

   _____

   _____

5. Jamison has 70 square feet of plywood to make a floor for a two-room clubhouse he is building. The floor of one room is 8 feet long and 6 feet wide. The floor of the other room is 5 feet long and 4 feet wide. How can he decide if he has enough plywood?

   _____

   _____

6. Amy wants to make a frame for a painting that is 24 inches long and 18 inches wide. She found a wood molding she would like to use. How can she decide how much molding she needs to make the frame?

   _____

44

Name _____ Date _____

Homework Practice

Select Appropriate Measurement Formulas

Determine whether you need to find the perimeter, area, or volume. Then solve.

1. Charlene is filling a box planter with soil. Each bag of soil contains enough to fill 500 cubic inches. If the base of the box planter is a 9-inch square and the sides are 18 inches tall, how many bags of soil will Charlene need?

   _____

2. Tobias is helping his uncle paint the side of a barn. Each can of paint covers 80 square feet. If the side of the barn is 10 feet high and 15 feet wide, how many cans of paint will Tobias need?

   _____

3. Gina is tying up a stack of newspapers with string. She wants the string to wrap around twice, once lengthwise and once crosswise. If the stack of newspapers is 11 inches wide, 13 inches long, and 15 inches high, how much string will she need?

   _____

Spiral Review

Find the surface area of each prism. (Lesson 14–7)

4.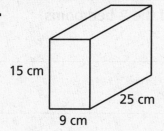

   15 cm   25 cm   9 cm

5.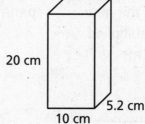

   20 cm   10 cm   5.2 cm

6.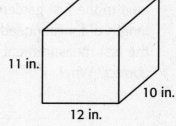

   11 in.   12 in.   10 in.

_____   _____   _____

Name _____ Date _____

Problem-Solving Practice

Select Appropriate Measurement Formulas

Solve.

1. Rita measured her living room floor to determine how many 12 in. by 12 in. tiles she needs to buy. Should she find the area or perimeter of the floor?

   _____

2. Nolan measured the 4 sides of his garden. His garden is 20 ft long and 10 ft wide. How much garden fencing will he need to place around his garden? Did you use area or perimeter to find your answer?

   _____

3. Bobby measures a room that is 9 ft wide and 15 ft long. He needs to decide how much carpet to buy. How many square feet of carpeting does he need?

   _____

4. Nan wants to fill a canister with raisins. Would she need to find the area, perimeter, or volume of the canister to determine the amount of raisins that will fit?

   _____

5. Reggie is planting vegetables in a rectangular garden. The space measures 12 ft by 5 ft. He figured out how many feet of fencing he would need to go around the garden. He then decides to double the area. Reggie digs another rectangle with the same measurements next to the first garden. To find the new length of fencing needed, he multiplied the first measurement by 2. Is this correct? Why?

   _____

   _____

6. Leah and Alison have bedrooms with the same area, but different dimensions. Leah's bedroom measures 9 ft wide, and has a length 7 ft longer than the width. What are the possible dimensions of Alison's bedroom? What is the difference between the perimeters of the 2 bedrooms?

   _____

   _____

   _____

   _____

Name _____ Date _____

Enrich

Choose an Appropriate Tool and Unit

Solve.

1. A punch is made from 3 pints of orange juice and 1 pint of lemonade.

   a. Will the punch fit in a punch bowl with a capacity of 2 quarts? Explain.

   _____

   b. Will the punch fit in a bowl with a capacity of 7 cups? Explain.

   _____

2. A box is $9\frac{1}{2}$ inches long, $6\frac{3}{4}$ inches wide, and $2\frac{5}{8}$ inches deep.

   a. Will a model that is $1\frac{1}{2}$ inches tall, $6\frac{5}{8}$ inches wide, and $9\frac{3}{16}$ inches long fit inside the box? Explain.

   _____

   b. Will a model that is $2\frac{3}{4}$ inches tall, $9\frac{5}{8}$ inches long, and $6\frac{3}{4}$ inches wide fit inside the box? Explain.

   _____

3. Luisa and Dolores are running in a 100-yard race.

   a. What is an appropriate unit of measurement and measurement tool to use to measure their race times? Explain.

   _____

   b. Is it likely that their race times will be recorded to the nearest minute? Explain.

   _____

4. A 7-year-old child visits a doctor for a checkup.

   a. What is an appropriate unit of measurement and measurement tool to use to measure the weight of the child? Explain.

   _____

   b. What is an appropriate unit of measurement and measurement tool to use to measure the height of the child? Explain.

   _____

Name _____ Date _____

Reteach

Problem-Solving Investigation: Choose the Best Strategy

Alberto often goes along with his sister, Sonia, to videotape her soccer games. He records each $1\frac{1}{2}$ hour game. If she played 11 games, would Alberto be able to fit all her games on one DVD if each DVD holds 15 hours of video?

Step 1 Understand	**Be sure you understand the problem.** Alberto will videotape Sonia's soccer games. Each game is $1\frac{1}{2}$ hours. Sonia played 11 games. The DVD will hold 15 hours of video.
Step 2 Plan • Make a model • Draw a diagram • Look for a pattern	**Make a plan.** Choose a strategy. You can draw a diagram. Draw a line segment that is 15 inches long. Then mark intervals that are $1\frac{1}{2}$ inches long. Count the intervals to see whether you have 11 intervals.
Step 3 Solve	**Carry out your plan.** Two games take 3 hours. So, in 15 hours Alberto can fit 2×5 or 10 games on his DVD. So 11 games will *not* fit on one DVD.
Step 4 Check	**Is the solution reasonable?** Reread the problem. How can you check your answers?

Reteach

Problem-Solving Investigation: Choose the Best Strategy
(continued)

Use any strategy shown below to solve each problem.

• Make a model   • Draw a diagram   • Look for a pattern   • Use logical reasoning

1. Mitchell spent some money on his haircut. He paid the cashier three $5-bills. He received $4.25 back from the cashier. How much did he pay for the haircut?

_____

2. Callie is throwing a party and spends a total of $135. She spends $20 on cake, $40 on food, and $25 for decorations. If the rest of the money was spent on music, how much did the music cost?

_____

3. Meredith spent $125 on new clothes. She also purchased school supplies that totaled $45. She received 10% back on her total purchase. How much did she receive back?

_____

4. Jordan works at a pool during the week. Monday he worked for 30 minutes, Tuesday he worked for 40 minutes, Wednesday he worked for 50 minutes. If the pattern continues, how long will he work on Friday?

_____

5. Roberto is looking for the better deal on a bag of pens. One bag has 6 pens for $3.65. Another bag is $4.98 for 8 pens. Which one should Roberto buy?

_____

14-9

Skills Practice

Problem-Solving Investigation: Choose the Best Strategy

Use any strategy shown below to solve each problem.

- Make a model
- Draw a diagram
- Look for a pattern
- Use logical reasoning

1. A pet store is building new cages for their birds. They have 8 cockatiels, 32 parakeets, and 28 finches. How many cages will they need if each cage will hold either 2 cockatiels, 10 parakeets, or 14 finches. The different types of birds are all kept separate.

_____

2. You decide to do an even exchange on an outfit that you received for your birthday. The top and pants total $32. If you pick another top for $14, how much is the highest price of the pants, that you can pick out?

_____

3. Danielle picks fruit from her family's lemon tree. She picked 28 lemons. If each lemon makes $\frac{1}{2}$ cup of lemonade after adding water, how many cups of lemonade can she make?

_____

4. Meredith is making a dress. She has 5 feet of ribbon. She needs 12 inches of ribbon for the neck and two 6-inch pieces for the cuffs. How many cuts will she need to make to get 6 equal lengths from the rest of the ribbon for bows?

_____

5. Taye ran for 3 miles each week. On each fourth week, he ran an extra mile. How many miles did he run after 4 weeks? How many miles did he run after 7 weeks?

_____

Name _____ Date _____

Homework Practice

Problem-Solving Investigation: Choose the Best Strategy

Use any strategy shown below to solve each problem.

• Make a model   • Draw a diagram   • Look for a pattern   • Use logical reasoning

1. The Humane Society is building new cages for their dogs and cats. They have 2 crews of workers building them. There are 28 dogs and 34 cats. All the animals are kept separate. The first crew can build a cage in 1 hour and the second crew, which is smaller, takes 2 hours to build a cage. How many hours will it take to build the cages using both crews if they do not take a break?

_____

2. You are shopping for some new clothes. You buy a shirt for $28 and a pair of dress shoes for $45. If you give the cashier a $100 bill, how much change will you get back?

_____

3. Marge needs to bake 8 dozen cookies for a bake sale. For each batch of cookies she needs $4\frac{1}{2}$ cups of flour. Each batch makes 2 dozen cookies. How much flour does she need?

_____

Spiral Review

Determine whether you need to find the perimeter, area, or volume. Then solve.   **(Lesson 14–8)**

4. Mr. Bauer wants to enclose his rectangular garden with a fence. If the garden measures 12 feet by 9 feet, how many feet of fencing will he need to buy?

_____

5. Jameson has a storage bin that is the shape of a cube for his building blocks. If one side of the cube measures 2 feet, how many cubic feet of space does he have for storage?

_____

Name _____ Date _____

Enrich

Perimeter and Area Problem-Solving

Solve. Explain how you found your solution.

1. Nick builds the box shown at the right. The top of the box is mahogany. The sides and bottom are pine. How much mahogany does Nick use?

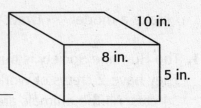

_____

_____

2. Jenny's pool is surrounded by square tiles that are each 2 feet by 2 feet. She needs a cover for her pool. How many square feet must the cover be? Explain.

Each ☐ is 2 ft by 2 ft.

_____

_____

_____

3. The park to the right is a field of grass with a diagonal path that is made of gravel. Workers have put gates at each end of the path. The rest of the park will be surrounded by a fence. How many meters of fencing are needed?

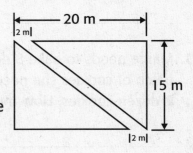

_____

_____

_____

4. A garden covers 36 square feet. What is the least amount of fence that could be used to enclose a garden of this size?

_____

_____

_____

Name _____ Date _____

Individual Progress Checklist

Learning Mastery			Lesson	Lesson Goal	Comments
B	**D**	**M**			
			14-1	Find the perimeters of polygons.	
			14-2	Find and estimate the areas of figures by counting squares.	
			14-3	Find the areas of rectangles.	
			14-4	Identify characteristics of three-dimensional figures.	
			14-5	Solve problems by making a model.	
			14-6	Find the volumes of rectangular prisms.	
			14-7	Find the surface areas of rectangular prisms.	
			14-8	Select and use appropriate units and formulas to measure length, perimeter, area, and volume.	
			14-9	Choose the best strategy to solve a problem.	

B = Beginning; **D** = Developing; **M** = Mastered

Note to Parents

_____

_____

_____

_____

_____

Assessment

14

Chapter Diagnostic Test

Add.

1. $3 + 11 + 16$

2. $5 + 12 + 13$

3. $6\frac{1}{4} + 7\frac{1}{4}$

4. $4.2 + 5.6 + 27.3$

5. Mr. Ramos bought two bottles of juice and two fruit trays for the birthday party. If each bottle of juice cost $5.99 and each fruit tray cost $23, how much did Mr. Ramos spend?

Multiply.

6. 14×8

7. 26×3

8. $2 \times 6 \times 7$

9. $3 \times 16 \times 12$

10. $14 \times 17 \times 6$

11. $2(14 + 10)$

12. $(3)(2)(4) + (3)(2)(8) + (3)(4)(8)$

13. $(4)(6)(5) + (4)(6)(3) + (4)(5)(3)$

14. Rita bought six packages of banana bread mix. Each mix makes 12 muffins. If Rita sells each muffin for $3, what is the most she could earn?

1. _____

2. _____

3. _____

4. _____

5. _____

6. _____

7. _____

8. _____

9. _____

10. _____

11. _____

12. _____

13. _____

14. _____

14 Chapter Pretest

Find the perimeter of each square or rectangle.

1.

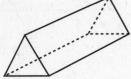

13 in.

4 in.

2.

13 ft

13 ft

1. _____

2. _____

Describe the parts that are parallel and congruent. Then identify the figure.

3.

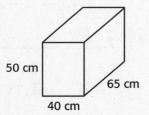

3. _____

Find the volume of each rectangular prism.

4.

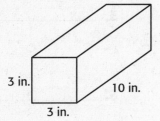

3 in.

10 in.

3 in.

5.

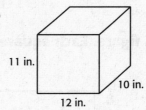

11 in.

10 in.

12 in.

4. _____

5. _____

6.

50 cm

65 cm

40 cm

7.

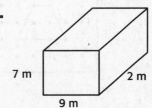

7 m

2 m

9 m

6. _____

7. _____

Name _____ Date _____

Quiz 1 *(Lessons 14–1 through 14–3)*

Find the perimeter of each square or rectangle.

1.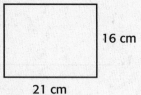
16 cm
21 cm

2.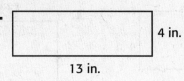
4 in.
13 in.

3.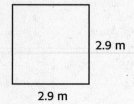
2.9 m
2.9 m

4.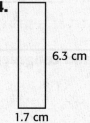
6.3 cm
1.7 cm

Find the area of each rectangle.

5.
10 in.
25 in.

6.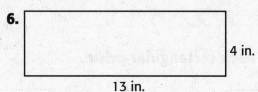
4 in.
13 in.

Estimate the area of each figure. Each square represents 1 square centimeter.

7.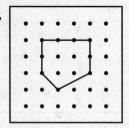

8.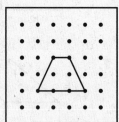

1. _____

2. _____

3. _____

4. _____

5. _____

6. _____

7. _____

8. _____

Name _____ Date _____

Quiz 2 *(Lessons 14–4 through 14–6)*

Find the volume of each rectangular prism.

1.

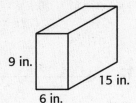

9 in.

15 in.

6 in.

2.

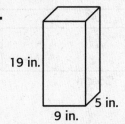

19 in.

5 in.

9 in.

3.

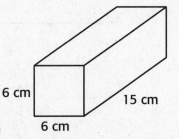

6 cm

15 cm

6 cm

4. What is the volume of a rectangular box that has a base area of 75 inches and a height of 20 inches?

1. _____

2. _____

Describe parts of each figure that are parallel and congruent. Then identify the figure.

5.

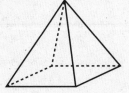

3. _____

4. _____

Solve. Use the *make a model* strategy.

6. Sumi wants to wear something nice for her first day of school. She picks out a purple top, a red top, and a green top along with jeans and black pants. She also has tennis shoes or dress shoes to choose from. How many combinations can she choose from?

5. _____

6. _____

7. Mark is building a desk. He has a space of 10 feet by 9 feet for his desk. His desk has 2 parts. The first piece of his desk has a work surface that is 9 feet by 5 feet. The second part of the desk is 3 feet by 3 feet and one side is placed up against one of the larger sides of the work surface. Will the desk fit in the space that he has available?

7. _____

Name _____ Date _____

Quiz 3 *(Lessons 14–7 through 14–9)*

Find the surface area of each rectangular prism.

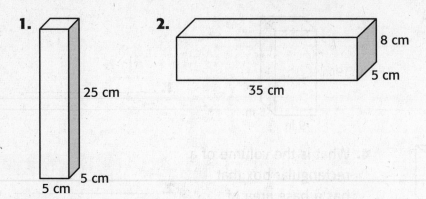

1. _____

2. _____

Determine whether you need to find the perimeter, area, or volume. Then solve.

3. Margaret is painting the fence that runs along one side of her yard. It is 5 feet high and 20 feet long. How much space is she painting?

3. _____

4. John Paul is putting a border around a quilt. The quilt is 65 inches wide and 96 inches long. How much border fabric will he need?

4. _____

5. A kitchen floor is 10 feet wide by 14 feet long. New tile for the floor cost $8 per square foot. How much would it cost to re-tile the floor?

5. _____

Use any strategy to solve.

6. A survey was taken on people's favorite color. 45 people liked red best, 25 chose blue, and 30 liked yellow. What fraction of people liked red?

6. _____

7. A train goes around its track every 3 minutes. How many times does it go around in 1 hour? In 24 hours?

7. _____

Name _____ Date _____

Mid-Chapter Test *(Lessons 14–1 through 14–3)*

Find the perimeter of each square or rectangle.

1.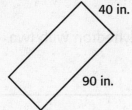
40 in.
90 in.

2.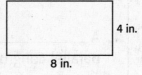
4 in.
8 in.

3.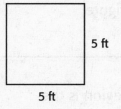
5 ft
5 ft

4.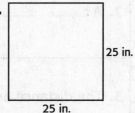
25 in.
25 in.

1. _____

2. _____

3. _____

4. _____

Estimate the area of each figure. Each square represents 1 square centimeter.

5.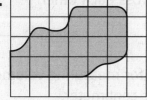

6.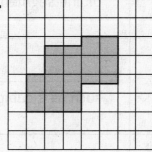

5. _____

6. _____

Find the area of each rectangle.

7.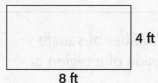
4 ft
8 ft

8.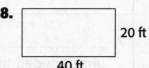
20 ft
40 ft

7. _____

8. _____

Name _____ Date _____

Vocabulary Test

Match each word to its definition. Write your answers on the lines provided.

area	**1.** A _____ is a polyhedron with two parallel congruent faces.
cone	**2.** A _____ is a solid figure.
cubic units	**3.** The distance around a shape or region is the _____ .
rectangular prism	**4.** A _____ is a closed figure made up of line segments that do not cross each other.
polygon	**5.** _____ are units for measuring volume, such as a cubic inch or a cubic centimeter.
prism	**6.** A _____ is a solid that has a circular base and one curved surface from the base to a vertex.
three-dimensional figure	**7.** _____ is the number of square units needed to cover the inside of a region or plane figure.
perimeter	**8.** _____ is a three-dimensional object in which all 6 faces are rectangular.

Name _____ Date _____

Oral Assessment

Use construction paper to cut out 3 rectangles of different sizes and label them A–C. Use a ruler to measure the length and width in centimeters for each rectangle. Label each rectangle with its corresponding height and width.

Read each question aloud to the student. Then write the student's answers on the lines below the question.

1. What is the area and perimeter of the rectangle A?

_____

2. What is the area and perimeter of rectangle B?

_____

3. What is the area and perimeter of rectangle C?

_____

4. Explain your answers.

_____

5. Which rectangle has the smallest area and perimeter?

_____

6. Justify your answer.

_____

_____

7. What rectangle would have the largest surface area if they all had a width of 1 inch?

_____

Assessment

Draw and label a parallelogram with a base of 8 inches and a height of 7 inches on the board.

Read each question aloud to the student. Then write the student's answer on the lines below the question.

8. How does the area of this parallelogram relate to the area of a rectangle with a length of 8 inches and a width of 7 inches?

_____

9. What is the area of the parallelogram?

_____

Draw and label a triangle with a base of 10 inches and a height of 6 inches on the board.

Read each question aloud to the student. Then write the student's answer on the lines below the question.

10. How does the area of a triangle relate to the area of a parallelogram?

_____

11. What is the area of the triangle?

_____

Name _____ Date _____

Chapter Project Rubric

Assessment

Score	Explanation
3	Student successfully completed the chapter project.
	Student demonstrated appropriate use of chapter information in completing the chapter project.
2	Student completed the chapter project with partial success.
	Student partially demonstrated appropriate use of chapter information in completing the chapter project.
1	Student did not complete the chapter project or completed it with little success.
	Student demonstrated very little appropriate use of chapter information in completing the chapter project.
0	Student did not complete the chapter project.
	Student demonstrated inappropriate use of chapter information in completing the chapter project.

Foldables® Rubric

Measure Perimeter, Area, and Volume

Three-Pocket Foldable

Score	Explanation
3	Student properly assembled Foldables® graphic organizer according to instructions.
	Student recorded information related to the chapter in the manner directed by the Foldables graphic organizer.
	Student used the Foldables graphic organizer as a study guide and organizational tool.
2	Student exhibited partial understanding of proper Foldables graphic organizer assembly.
	Student recorded most but not all information related to the chapter in the manner directed by the Foldables graphic organizer.
	Student demonstrated partial use of the Foldables graphic organizer as a study guide and organizational tool.
1	Student showed little understanding of proper Foldables graphic organizer assembly.
	Student recorded only some information related to the chapter in the manner directed by the Foldables graphic organizer.
	Student demonstrated little use of the Foldables graphic organizer as a study guide and organizational tool.
0	Student did not assemble Foldables graphic organizer according to instructions.
	Student recorded little or no information related to the chapter in the manner directed by the Foldables graphic organizer.
	Student did not use the Foldables graphic organizer as a study guide and organizational tool.

Name _____ Date _____

Chapter Test, Form 1

Read each question carefully. Write your answer on the line provided.

1. Estimate the area of the figure.

   A. 10 square units **C.** 13 square units
   B. 11.5 square units **D.** 15 square units

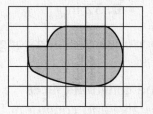

1. _____

2. Find the perimeter.

   F. 51.6 m **H.** 68.8 m
   G. 86 m **J.** 103.2 m

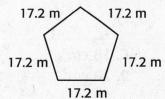

2. _____

3. Estimate the area.

   A. 14 square yards **C.** 21 square yards
   B. 20 square yards **D.** 28 square yards

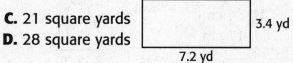

3. _____

4. Find the volume.

   F. 31.5 m³ **H.** 90 m³
   G. 45 m³ **J.** 135 m³

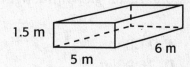

4. _____

5. Find the surface area.

   A. 220 cm² **C.** 180 cm²
   B. 177 cm² **D.** 208 cm²

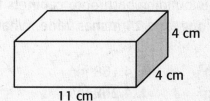

5. _____

6. Find the surface area.

   F. 500 cm² **H.** 384 cm²
   G. 410 cm² **J.** 390 cm²

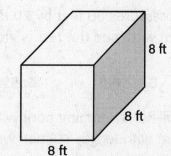

6. _____

Name _____ Date _____

Chapter Test, Form 1   (continued)

7. Find the area.

   A. 48 in²   **C.** 24 in²

   B. 12 in²   **D.** 32 in²

   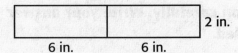

   2 in.

   6 in.   6 in.

   7. _____

8. Find the number of parallel and congruent sides a can of soup has.

   F. none

   G. 2 parallel and congruent faces

   H. 2 pairs of parallel and congruent faces

   J. 4 parallel and congruent faces

   8. _____

9. Find the area.

   A. 9 cm²   **C.** 18 cm²

   B. 10 cm²   **D.** 20 cm²

   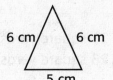

   4 cm

   5 cm

   9. _____

10. Find the perimeter.

    F. 180 cm   **H.** 34 cm

    G. 68 cm   **J.** 17 cm

    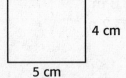

    6 cm   6 cm

    5 cm

    10. _____

11. Find the perimeter of a rectangle with length 3.8 inches and height 7.1 inches.

    A. 19.6 in.   **C.** 21.8 in.

    B. 20.8 in.   **D.** 26.98 in.

    11. _____

12. Samantha is building bathroom cabinets that are 36 inches high, 12 inches long, and 24 inches wide. What is the surface area of the cabinets?

    F. 3,168 in²   **H.** 4,168 in²

    G. 3,268 in²   **J.** 4,268 in²

    12. _____

13. Saul's front yard measures 50 feet by 20 feet. His driveway takes up 350 ft² of the front yard, and the rest is grass. How much grass is in Saul's front yard?

    A. 1,000 ft²   **B.** 650 ft²   **C.** 550 ft²   **D.** 350 ft²

    13. _____

14. Emma needs to fill her swimming pool with water. Her pool is a rectangular prism with length 10 feet, width 7 feet, and height 6 feet. How much water does Emma need to fill her pool?

    F. 420 ft³   **G.** 840 ft³   **H.** 460 ft³   **J.** 820 ft³

    14. _____

Name _____ Date _____

Chapter Test, Form 2A

Read each question carefully. Write your answer on the line provided.

1. Find the number of parallel and congruent sides a traffic cone has.

   A. none
   B. 2 parallel and congruent faces
   C. 2 pairs of parallel and congruent faces
   D. 4 parallel and congruent faces

   1. _____

2. Find the perimeter.

   F. 38.1 m   **H.** 63.5 m
   G. 50.8 m   **J.** 161.29 m

   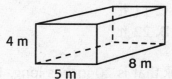

   2. _____

3. Find the area.

   A. 18 in²   **C.** 27 in²
   B. 26 in²   **D.** 36 in²

   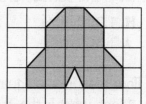

   3. _____

4. Find the volume.

   F. 175 m³   **H.** 80 m³
   G. 160 m³   **J.** 28 m³

   4 m
   5 m   8 m

   4. _____

5. Estimate the area of the figure.

   A. 10 square units   **C.** 13 square units
   B. 12 square units   **D.** 13.5 square units

   5. _____

6. Find the surface area.

   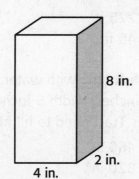

   8 in.
   2 in.
   4 in.

   6. _____

Name _____ Date _____

Chapter Test, Form 2A *(continued)*

7. Find the area.

   A. 60 m²   **C.** 25 m²

   B. 30 m²   **D.** 15 m²

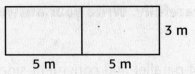

3 m

5 m   5 m

7. _____

8. Find the volume.

   F. 31 cu in.   **H.** 1,320 cu in.

   G. 1,230 cu in.   **J.** 1,420 cu in.

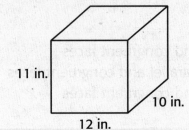

11 in.

10 in.

12 in.

8. _____

9. Find the area.

   A. 10 in²   **C.** 16 in²

   B. 12 in²   **D.** 18 in²

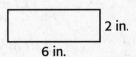

2 in.

6 in.

9. _____

10. Find the perimeter.

    F. 28 cm   **H.** 16 cm

    G. 24 cm   **J.** 14 cm

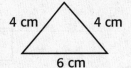

4 cm   4 cm

6 cm

10. _____

11. Find the perimeter of a rectangle with base 1.2 feet and height 4.3 feet.

    A. 5.5 ft   **C.** 11 ft

    B. 10 ft   **D.** 22 ft

11. _____

12. Josie has a fish tank that is 20 inches long, 15 inches tall and 10 inches wide. What is the surface area of the fish tank?

    F. 1,100 in²   **H.** 1,200 in²

    G. 1,250 in²   **J.** 1,300 in²

12. _____

13. The total area of a floor plan is 320 square feet. If the kitchen measures 5 feet by 9 feet, what is the area of the rest of the floor plan?

    A. 595 ft²   **C.** 275 ft²

    B. 298 ft²   **D.** 45 ft²

13. _____

14. Traci wants to fill her fish tank with water. The tank is a rectangular prism with length 12 inches, width 5 inches, and height 7 inches. How much water does Traci need to fill her fish tank?

    F. 420 in³   **H.** 460 in³

    G. 840 in³   **J.** 820 in³

14. _____

Name _____ Date _____

Chapter Test, Form 2B

Read each question carefully. Write your answer on the line provided.

Find the perimeter of each figure.

1.

15 in.

18 in.

   A. 23 in.   **B.** 33 in.   **C.** 66 in.   **1.** _____

2. 12.7 m   12.7 m

12.7 m   12.7 m

12.7 m

   F. 38.1 m   **G.** 50.8   **H.** 63.5 m   **2.** _____

3.

4 cm   4 cm

6 cm

   A. 28 cm   **B.** 16 cm   **C.** 14 cm   **3.** _____

4. rectangle

$\ell = 1.2$ ft, $w = 4.3$ ft

   F. 5.5 ft   **G.** 11 ft   **H.** 22 ft   **4.** _____

Find the area of each figure.

5.

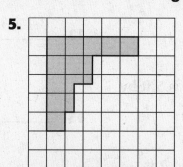

   A. 10 square units   **C.** 12 square units
   B. 14 square units   **5.** _____

Name _____ Date _____

Chapter Test, Form 2B *(continued)*

6. **A.** 180 cm²   **C.** 60 cm²
    B. 80 cm²   **D.** 36 cm²

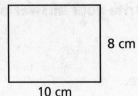

6. _____

7. **A.** 60 m²   **C.** 25 m²
    B. 30 m²   **D.** 15 m²

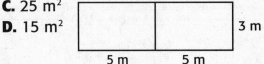

7. _____

8. Find the surface area.

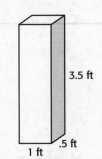

8. _____

Find the volume of each figure.

9. **A.** 160 m³   **B.** 80 m³   **C.** 28 m³

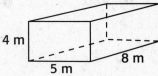

9. _____

10. rectangular prism
    $\ell = 4$ mi, $w = 4$ mi, $h = 4$ mi

    F. 64 mi³   **G.** 56 mi³   **H.** 48 mi³

10. _____

11. rectangular prism
    $\ell = 9$ m, $w = 40$ m, $h = 1.5$ m

    A. 540 m³   **B.** 450 m³   **C.** 270 m³

11. _____

12. How many parallel and congruent sides does a triangular prism have?
    A. none
    B. 2 parallel and congruent faces
    C. 2 pairs of parallel and congruent faces
    D. 4 parallel and congruent faces

12. _____

13. The area of an apartment is 475 square feet. If the kitchen is 5 ft by 9 ft, what is the area of the rest of the apartment?
    A. 430 ft²   **B.** 275 ft²   **C.** 45 ft²

13. _____

14. Molly is building an animal pen that is 6 ft long, 3 ft tall and 2 ft wide. What is the surface area of the animal pen?
    F. 70 ft²   **G.** 72 ft²   **H.** 74 ft²

14. _____

Chapter Test, Form 2C

Assessment

Read each question carefully. Write your answer on the line provided.

1. Find the volume.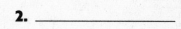

4 m / 5 m / 8 m

1. _____

2. Find the number of parallel and congruent sides an ice cream cone has.

2. _____

3. Find the volume.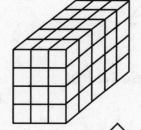

3. _____

4. Find the area.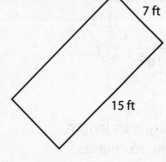

7 ft / 15 ft

4. _____

5. Find the area.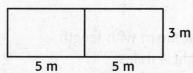

3 m / 5 m / 5 m

5. _____

6. Find the surface area.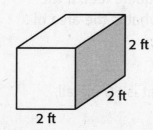

2 ft / 2 ft / 2 ft

6. _____

7. Find the perimeter.

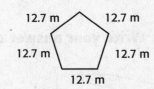

7. _____

8. Estimate the area of the figure.

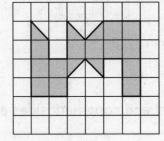

8. _____

9. Find the perimeter.

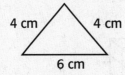

9. _____

10. Find the perimeter of a rectangle with base 1.2 feet and height 4.3 feet.

10. _____

11. Find the perimeter.

15 in.

18 in.

11. _____

12. Find the volume of a rectangular prism with length 11 meters, width 4 meters, and height 15 meters.

12. _____

13. Find the volume of a rectangular prism with length 7 miles, width 6 miles, and height 4 miles.

13. _____

14. The total area of a floor plan is 500 square feet. If the kitchen measures 5 feet by 11 feet, what is the area of the rest of the floor plan?

14. _____

15. What is the surface area of a crate that is 50 in. tall, 30 in. wide, and 15 in. long?

15. _____

Name _____ Date _____

Chapter Test, Form 2D

Read each question carefully. Write your answer on the line provided.

1. _____

Find the perimeter.

1.

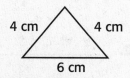

15 in.

18 in.

2. rectangle
$b = 1.2$ ft, $h = 4.3$ ft

2. _____

3.

4 cm   4 cm

6 cm

4.

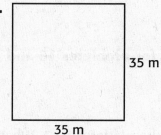

12.7 m   12.7 m

12.7 m   12.7 m

12.7 m

3. _____

Find the area.

5.

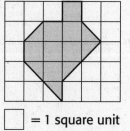

☐ = 1 square unit

6.

35 m

35 m

4. _____

5. _____

6. _____

Find the surface area.

7.

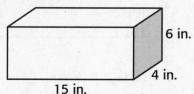

6 in.

4 in.

15 in.

8.

11 cm

3 cm

5 cm

7. _____

9.

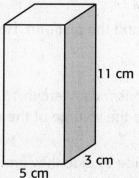

4 cm

4 cm

4 cm

8. _____

9. _____

Find the volume.

10. rectangular prism

    $\ell = 9$ m, $w = 4$ m, $h = 1.5$ m

    10. _____

11.

    4 m

    5 m   8 m

    11. _____

12. rectangular prism

    $\ell = 8$ mi, $w = 4$ mi, $h = 7$ mi

    12. _____

13. Find the number of parallel and congruent sides a triangular prism has.

    13. _____

Use the following information for problems 16 and 17.

Jose builds a 6 ft by 8 ft platform.

14. Jose multiplies each side of the platform by 2. What is the area of the new platform?

    14. _____

15. Jose wants to put a railing around the platform. He should measure the _____.

    15. _____

16. Robert's pool is a rectangular prism with length 15 ft, width 8 ft, and height 5 ft. Find the volume of the pool.

    16. _____

17. Josh is building two cabinets side by side they are each 2 feet tall, 1.5 feet long, and 1 foot wide. What is their total surface area?

    17. _____

Name _____ Date _____

Chapter Test, Form 3

Read each question carefully. Write your answer on the line provided.

Find the area of each figure.

1.

12 cm   *z*

2.

42 cm

35 cm

3.

2 ft

11 ft

4.

18 ft

r

1. _____

2. _____

3. _____

4. _____

Find the volume of each figure.

5.

12 cm

15 cm

7 cm

6.

3 in.   16 in.

1 in.

5. _____

6. _____

Find the surface area of the figure.

7.

15 in.

5 in.

10 in.

7. _____

75

Name _____ Date _____

Chapter Test, Form 3 *(continued)*

8. Find the number of parallel and congruent sides a rectangular prism has.

9. Estimate the area of the figure.

8. _____

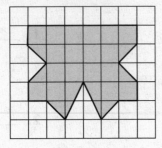

9. _____

Solve.

10. The perimeter of the rectangle is 30 in. What is the value of *p*?

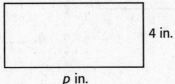

4 in.

p in.

10. _____

11. The area of the rectangle is 27 square inches. What is the value of *a*?

a

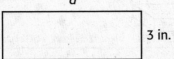

3 in.

11. _____

12. The volume of a piranha tank is 1,512 cubic meters. Given the information below, find the dimensions of the tank.

$\ell = (w + 2)$ m
$w = w$ m
$h = (w - 3)$ m

12. _____

13. Carly is painting her jewelry box and she needs to know how much paint to buy. If the box is 8 inches high, 7 inches wide and 4 inches long, what is the surface area?

13. _____

Name _____ Date _____

Chapter Extended-Response Test

Demonstrate your knowledge by giving a clear, concise solution to each problem. Be sure to include all relevant drawings and justify your answers. You may show your solution in more than one way or investigate beyond the requirements of the problem. If necessary, record your answer on another piece of paper.

1. In this chapter, you learned several ways to classify measurements, such as perimeter, area, and volume. How would you classify the measurements below? Explain your reasoning.

   a. the number of tiles needed to cover a kitchen floor

   b. the amount of sand in a sandbox

2. Explain, in words and symbols, how to find the measurements below.

   a. perimeter of a lawn that is 35 yards long and 10 yards wide

   b. area of a football pennant that is 3 feet long and measures 1.5 feet at the base

   c. area of a rectangle tile with a base 27 cm wide and a height of 1.5 cm

3. The table shows items that Felicity purchased at the supermarket. Answer each question below, using words and symbols.

Item	Length (cm)	Width (cm)	Height (cm)
Macaroni pasta	13	8	20
Cereal	19	6	25
Kosher salt	12	5	16
Green tea	10	10	10

   a. Which has more volume, a box of macaroni or a box of cereal?

   b. Felicity has a kitchen cabinet that can hold 15,000 cubic centimeters. About how many boxes of kosher salt she can store in it?

   c. What is the surface area of the macaroni pasta box? _____

Assessment

Name _____ Date _____

Cumulative Test Practice Chapters 1–14

Test Example

A paper clip bin has the dimensions shown. What is the volume of the paper clip bin?

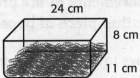

24 cm

8 cm

11 cm

A. 10 cubic centimeters   **C.** 2,112 cubic centimeters

B. 44 cubic centimeters   **D.** 2,000 cubic centimeters

Read the Question

You need to find the volume of the paper clip bin.

Solve the Question

Use the formula for the volume of a rectangular prism, $V = \ell wh$.

$V = \ell wh$	Volume of a rectangular prism
$V = 24 \times 11 \times 8$	Replace ℓ with 24, w with 11, and h with 8.
$V = 2{,}112$	Multiply

The volume of the paper clip container is 2,112 cubic centimeters. The answer is C.

Read each question carefully. Write your answer on the line provided.

1. Adrienne built a figure using centimeter cubes. The figure stood 8 cubes high and covered a 10-centimeter by 6-centimeter area of the floor. What is the volume of the figure?

A. 86 cm³   **C.** 480 cm³

B. 108 cm³   **D.** 1,332 cm³   **1.** _____

Cumulative Test Practice *(continued)*

2. The rectangular prism below has a length of 14 cm, a height of 4 cm and a width of 6 cm. What is the volume?

    F. 336 cm³   **H.** 2 cm³

    G. 24 cm³   **J.** 1, 231 cm³

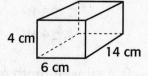

2. _____

3. Find the area of a rectangle with the sides measuring 5 feet, and 10 feet.

    A. 500 ft²   **B.** 100 ft²   **C.** 50 ft²   **D.** 30 ft²

3. _____

4. The side lengths and perimeters of regular polygons are shown in the table below. Which geometric figure is represented by the information in the table?

Side Length (inches)	Perimeter (inches)
3	18
5	30
8	48
10	60

4. _____

    F. hexagon   **H.** octagon

    G. triangle   **J.** pentagon

5. Mrs. Von Hagel designed a quilt by outlining trapezoids with ribbon as shown below. How much ribbon did Mrs. Von Hagel use to complete her quilt?

    A. 12 in.   **C.** 140 in.

    B. 20 in.   **D.** 144 in.

5. _____

P = 12 in.

Assessment

6. If the file cabinet is 2 ft tall, 3 ft long and 1 ft wide, what is its surface area?

   F. 22 ft²   **G.** 25 ft²

   H. 27 ft²   **J.** 24 ft²

   6. _____

7. Leena needs 4 cups of broth for a recipe. How many ounces of broth does she need?

   A. 16 ounces   **B.** 32 ounces   **C.** 40 ounces   **D.** 64 ounces

   7. _____

8. In the spreadsheet below, a formula applied to the values in columns A and B are the results in the values in column C. What is the formula?

	A	B	C
1	3	0	3
2	4	1	6
3	5	2	9
4	6	3	12

   F. C = A + B   **H.** C = A + 2B

   G. C = A − 2B   **J.** C = A − B

   8. _____

9. Ramon built a figure using centimeter cubes. The figure stood 10 cubes high and covered a 10-centimeter by 12-centimeter area of the floor. What is the volume of the figure?

   9. _____

10. Find the volume of a rectangular prism with sides measuring 6 feet, 7 feet and 14 feet.

   10. _____

11. Find the area of a rectangle with sides measuring 2 feet and 8 feet.

   11. _____

12. How many millimeters are equivalent to 100 centimeters?

   12. _____

13.   Are the figures congruent?

   13. _____

Name _____ Date _____

Student Recording Sheet

Use this recording sheet with pages 656–657 of the Student Edition.

Read each question. Then fill in the correct answer.

1. Ⓐ Ⓑ Ⓒ Ⓓ

2. Ⓕ Ⓖ Ⓗ Ⓙ

3. Ⓐ Ⓑ Ⓒ Ⓓ

4. Ⓕ Ⓖ Ⓗ Ⓙ

5. Ⓐ Ⓑ Ⓒ Ⓓ

6. Ⓕ Ⓖ Ⓗ Ⓙ

7. Ⓐ Ⓑ Ⓒ Ⓓ

8. Ⓕ Ⓖ Ⓗ Ⓙ

9. _____

10. _____

11. _____

_____

_____

12. _____

_____

_____

Answers (Graphic Organizer and Anticipation Guide)

14 Anticipation Guide

Measure Perimeter, Area, and Volume

STEP 1 · Before you begin Chapter 14

- Read each statement.
- Decide whether you agree (A) or disagree (D) with the statement.
- Write A or D in the first column OR if you are not sure whether you agree or disagree, write NS (not sure).

STEP 1 A, D, or NS	Statement	STEP 2 A or D
	1. A three-dimensional figure is a solid.	A
	2. Volume is the number of cubic units needed to fill a three-dimensional figure or solid figure.	A
	3. Area is the number of square units needed to cover the inside of a region or plane figure.	A
	4. Perimeter is the distance across a shape or a region.	D
	5. Perimeter and volume are the same measure.	D
	6. A triangular prism has triangular bases.	A

STEP 2 · After you complete Chapter 14

- Reread each statement and complete the last column by entering an A (agree) or a D (disagree).
- Did any of your opinions about the statements change from the first column?
- For those statements that you mark with a D, use a separate sheet of paper to explain why you disagree. Use examples, if possible.

---

14 Graphic Organizer

Use this graphic organizer to take notes on **Chapter 14: Measure Perimeter, Area, and Volume.** Fill in the missing sections of the graphic organizer.

Measurement	Formula	Example
perimeter of a square	$P = 4s$	The perimeter of a square with 7-inch sides is 4×7 inches. $P = 28$ inches.
perimeter of a rectangle	$P = 2\ell + 2w$	The perimeter of a rectangle with a length of 2 cm and a width of 5 cm is $(2 \times 2 \text{ cm}) + (2 \times 5 \text{ cm}) = 4 \text{ cm} + 10 \text{ cm}.$ $P = 14$ cm.
area of a rectangle	$A = \ell w$	The area of a rectangle with a length of 5 inches and a width of 3 inches is 5 in. $\times$ 3 in. $= 15$ square inches
area of a square	$A = s \times s$ or s^2	The area of a square with a 3-meter side is 3 meters $\times$ 3 meters. $A = 9$ square meters.
volume of a rectangular prism	$V = \ell w h$	The volume of a rectangular prism that is 4 inches long, 3 inches wide, and 5 inches high is 4 inches $\times$ 3 inches $\times$ 5 inches $= 60$ cubic inches. $V = 60$ in^3.

Chapter Resources

Answers

14–1 Skills Practice

Name _____ Date _____

Perimeters of Polygons

Find the perimeter of each figure.

1. 7 cm, 4 cm, 3 cm

14 cm

2. 5 m, 7 m

24 m

3. 4 in., 8 in., 5 in., 6 in., 10 in., 4 in.

37 in.

4. 3 cm, 3 cm, 3 cm, 5 cm

30 cm

5. 2 in., 2 in., 2 in., 6 in.

24 in.

6. 9 m, 9 m

36 m

Solve.

7. Find the perimeter of an isosceles triangle whose sides are 8 inches and whose base is 4 inches.

20 inches

8. Molly has 60 feet of fencing to go around the perimeter of her garden. She wants the garden to be a square. How long should each side be?

15 feet

Grade 5 — 9 — Chapter 14

14–1 Reteach

Name _____ Date _____

Perimeters of Polygons

Perimeter is the distance around a closed figure.

To find the perimeter of a figure, add the lengths of all the sides.

4 cm, 2 cm, 5 cm, 7 cm, 6 cm, 8 cm

$P = 6\ cm + 7\ cm + 4\ cm + 2\ cm + 5\ cm + 8\ cm$

$P = 32\ cm$

Find the perimeter of each figure.

1. 6 ft, 2 ft

16 ft

2. 7 cm, 3 cm

20 cm

3. 60 mm, 20 mm

160 mm

4. 2 m, 3 m, 3 m, 5 m, 2 m

15 m

5. 4 mm, 4 mm, 7 mm

15 mm

6. 4 cm, 4 cm, 4 cm

12 cm

7. 4 cm, 3 cm, 5 cm

12 cm

8. 2 in., 2 in.

8 in.

Grade 5 — 8 — Chapter 14

Answers (Lesson 14–1)

14–1

Name _____ Date _____

Problem-Solving Practice
Perimeters of Polygons

Solve.

1. Hannah wants to create a fenced enclosure for her dog. To figure out how much fencing she needs, Hannah made a drawing of the enclosure.

   5 m
   5 m

   How much fencing will she need?

   20 m

2. Johanna has a garden that is in the shape of a regular pentagon. Each side of the pentagon is 7 ft long. She decides to place a small, decorative wood fence around the perimeter. The fencing is sold in boxes of 5 pieces. Each piece has a length of 18 in. How many boxes of fencing will Johanna need to buy?

   5 boxes

3. A rectangular driveway is 40 ft long and 14 ft wide. What is the perimeter of the driveway?

   108 ft

4. Tara has a rectangular garden that is 10 ft long and 4 ft wide. She wants to put a small fence around it. If fencing costs $1.50 per ft, how much will the fence cost?

   $42

5. Vincent is designing a rectangular garden. The outside of the garden will measure 12 ft long and 5 ft wide. He plans to use tiles around the inside edge of the border. The tiles are squares, and each side measures 1 ft. After placing the tiles, Vincent will put a small fence around the inside, against the tiles. How many feet of fencing does he need?

   26 ft

14–1

Name _____ Date _____

Homework Practice
Perimeters of Polygons

Find the perimeter of each square or rectangle.

1.
   13 ft
   13 ft

   52 ft

2.
   4.76 m
   1.93 m

   13.38 m

3.
   11 ft
   $2\frac{1}{2}$ ft

   27 ft

4.
   4.8 m
   4.8 m

   19.2 m

5. Neil made a wooden, rectangular picture frame that is 14 inches long and 10 inches wide. If he charges $2.50 per foot, how much will he sell this frame for?

   $10.00

Spiral Review
(Lesson 13–9)

6. Create a pattern using transformations.

   Check students' work.

Answers

14-2

Name _____ Date _____

Reteach
Area

Area is the number of square units that cover the surface of a closed figure. One way to find the area of a figure is to use grid paper and count the number of square units.

There are 7 whole squares and 6 half squares.

The 6 half squares equal 3 whole squares.

The area of the figure is 10 square units.

When you cannot count square units or half square units exactly, you can estimate the area.

Step 1 Count the whole squares. There are 20 whole squares.

Step 2 Count the squares that are partly covered and divide that number by 2.

$8 \div 2 = 4$

Step 3 Add the numbers from Step 1 and Step 2.

$20 + 4 = 24$

The area of the figure is 24 square units.

☐ = 1 square unit

Estimate the area of each figure. Each square represents 1 square centimeter.

1.

$A = \underline{11}$ square centimeters

2.

$A = \underline{13\frac{1}{2}}$ square centimeters

3.

$A = \underline{16}$ square centimeters

Grade 5   13   Chapter 14

14-1

Name _____ Date _____

Enrich
Perimeter of Rectangles

Play this game with a partner. Take turns.

How to Play

• Toss two 1–6 number cubes. Use the two numbers rolled to form a 2-digit number.

• If possible, draw a rectangle on the grid below that has as many units in its perimeter as the two-digit number rolled. Write your initials in it. Your rectangle may not overlap another rectangle.

• When the number cubes have been rolled four consecutive times without a rectangle being drawn, the game is over.

The player who draws more rectangles wins.

Describe a strategy you and your partner used to play this game. **Answers may vary. Possible answer: First we drew narrow rectangles scattered throughout the game board to leave places that would be too small for the others to draw rectangles in as the game progressed.**

Grade 5   12   Chapter 14

14–2

Name _____ Date _____

Homework Practice
Area

Chapter Resources

Estimate the area of each figure. Each square represents 1 square centimeter.

1. **17 cm²**

2. **16 cm²**

3. **19 cm²**

4. **10 cm²**

5. **22 cm²**

6. **24 cm²**

Spiral Review

Find the perimeter of each square or rectangle. (Lesson 14–1)

7. 3 m, 3 m — **12 m**

8. 9 in., 4 in. — **26 in.**

9. 7 yd, 3 yd — **20 yds**

14–2

Name _____ Date _____

Skills Practice
Area

Estimate the area of each figure. Each square represents 1 square centimeter.

1. A = **23 cm²**

2. A = **16 cm²**

3. **15.5 cm²**

4. A = **19 cm²**

5. A = **20 cm²**

6. $18\frac{1}{2}$ **cm²**

7. A = **14 cm²**

8. A = $25\frac{1}{2}$ **cm²**

9. A = **12 cm²**

Answers

Answers (Lesson 14–2)

14–2

Name _____ Date _____

Enrich

Perimeter and Area of Irregular Figures

You are a landscape designer. Your most recent project is a yard that measures 40 meters by 50 meters. You will include the features below.

- an irregularly-shaped pond that is between 100 and 200 square meters
- an irregularly-shaped vegetable garden that is between 50 and 100 square meters
- an irregularly-shaped flower garden that is between 50 and 100 square meters
- fences for the gardens
- a patio that is between 200 and 300 square meters

Sketch your design on the grid below. Include a scale that explains what each square represents. **Check students' drawings.**

How many feet of fencing do you need for the gardens? Explain how you found your answers. **Check students' answers.**

_____

Grade 5   17   Chapter 14

14–2

Name _____ Date _____

Problem-Solving Practice

Area

Solve. Use grid paper.

1. Dan has a kitchen countertop that runs the length of a 10-ft room and continues for 6 ft along another wall. The countertop is 2 ft wide. What is the area of the countertop?

   32 ft²

2. Denzel is toasting 4 bagels and 2 slices of bread. Each bagel is 4 inches in diameter. Each slice of bread has an area of 9 square inches. If the toaster oven rack is 8 inches by 11 inches, can he toast all the bagels and bread at the same time?

   yes

3. Pablo has 64 ft of fencing to enclose an area of his yard for a garden. Use grid paper to sketch different ways the fencing can exactly enclose an area. Determine the area of each and find out how he can use the 64 ft of fencing so that the garden will be the greatest area possible.

   The greatest area is a 16 ft by 16 ft square.

4. Regina needs to make a stop sign out of cardboard for the school play. She uses grid paper and a ruler to make a model of the sign. It is in the shape of an octagon. Each horizontal or vertical line equals three units on the grid. Each diagonal line goes diagonally across two units. Sketch the figure on grid paper. How many squares on the grid are included in the sign? **41** squares

   If each unit on the grid equals 4 in., how many square inches of cardboard will Regina need for the sign? **656 in²**

5. Mabel was helping her mother tile the kitchen floor. The size of the kitchen floor is 7 feet by 12 feet. The counters are 2 feet deep and run along the floor of one of the shorter walls. The refrigerator takes up another 6 square feet of floor space. If each tile is a 6-inch square, how many tiles are needed for the kitchen floor?

   256 tiles

6. Mai used grid paper to draw plans for a dog pen. She connected the following points in order: (1, 0), (1, 5), (4, 5), (4, 2), (6, 2), (6, 0), and (1, 0). The side of each square on the grid paper represents 2 ft of the dog pen. If Steve is covering the ground in Mai's dog pen with straw, how many square feet will he need to cover?

   40 ft

Grade 5   16   Chapter 14

Answers (Lesson 14-3)

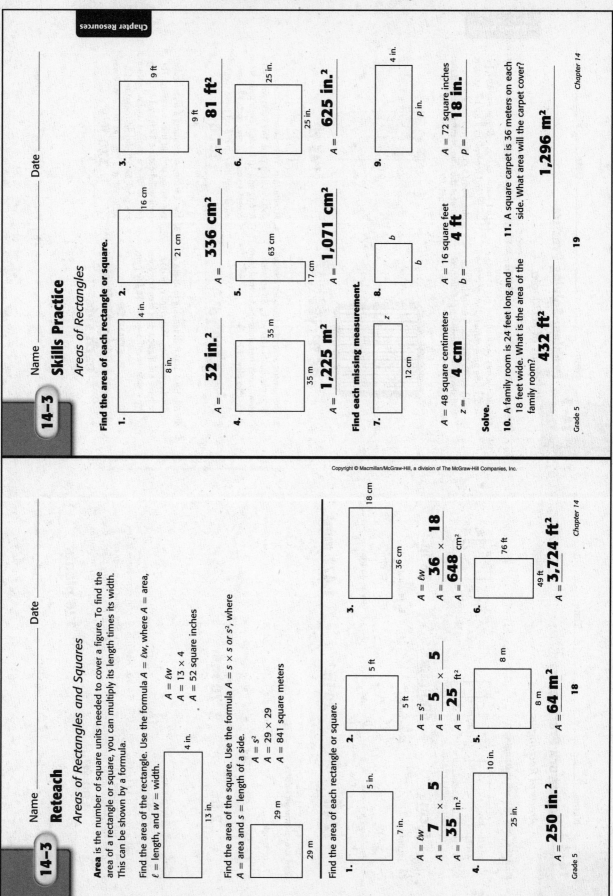

Skills Practice (14-3)

Areas of Rectangles

Find the area of each rectangle or square.

1. 8 in. × 4 in.
$A = $ **32 in.²**

2. 21 cm × 16 cm
$A = $ **336 cm²**

3. 9 ft × 9 ft
$A = $ **81 ft²**

4. 35 m × 35 m
$A = $ **1,225 m²**

5. 63 cm × 17 cm
$A = $ **1,071 cm²**

6. 25 in. × 25 in.
$A = $ **625 in.²**

Find each missing measurement.

7. z × 12 cm
$A = 48$ square centimeters
$z = $ **4 cm**

8. b × b
$A = 16$ square feet
$b = $ **4 ft**

9. p in. × 4 in.
$A = 72$ square inches
$p = $ **18 in.**

Solve.

10. A family room is 24 feet long and 18 feet wide. What is the area of the family room?
432 ft²

11. A square carpet is 36 meters on each side. What area will the carpet cover?
1,296 m²

Grade 5   19   Chapter 14

Reteach (14-3)

Areas of Rectangles and Squares

Area is the number of square units needed to cover a figure. To find the area of a rectangle or square, you can multiply its length times its width. This can be shown by a formula.

Find the area of the rectangle. Use the formula $A = \ell w$, where $A =$ area, $\ell =$ length, and $w =$ width.

13 in. × 4 in.
$A = \ell w$
$A = 13 \times 4$
$A = 52$ square inches

Find the area of the square. Use the formula $A = s \times s$ or s^2, where $A =$ area and $s =$ length of a side.

29 m × 29 m
$A = s^2$
$A = 29 \times 29$
$A = 841$ square meters

Find the area of each rectangle or square.

1. 7 in. × 5 in.
$A = \ell w$
$A = \underline{7} \times \underline{5}$
$A = \underline{35}$ in.²

2. 5 ft × 5 ft
$A = s^2$
$A = \underline{5} \times \underline{5}$
$A = \underline{25}$ ft²

3. 36 cm × 18 cm
$A = \ell w$
$A = \underline{36} \times \underline{18}$
$A = \underline{648}$ cm²

4. 25 in. × 10 in.
$A = $ **250 in.²**

5. 8 m × 8 m
$A = $ **64 m²**

6. 49 ft × 76 ft
$A = $ **3,724 ft²**

Grade 5   18   Chapter 14

Answers (Lesson 14–3)

14-3

Name _____ Date _____

Problem-Solving Practice
Areas of Rectangles

Solve.

1. Felicia wants to clean the rug in her room. She buys carpet cleaner that will clean 40 ft². Find the area of her rug. Will she have enough carpet cleaner?

6 ft
6 ft

36 ft²; yes

2. Lori wants to buy a flower mat that has seeds and fertilizer in it for her garden. She made a diagram of her garden. What is the area of the flower mat that she needs?

9 ft
5 ft

45 ft²

3. The playing area of a college's football field measures 100 yd by 53 yd wide. How much area does the football team have to play on?

5,300 yd²

4. Mr. and Mrs. Wilkes want to make a patio in their yard. The patio will be 15 ft long and 10 ft wide. Each patio stone covers 1 square ft and costs $2. How much will they spend on patio tiles?

$300

5. You have 100 ft of fencing to make a pen for your dog. You want your dog to have the biggest play area possible. What shape would you make the pen?

a square measuring 25 ft on each side

6. The Carsons are putting a rectangular swimming pool in their backyard. The pool will measure 20 by 12 ft. They plan to have a cement walkway around the pool, which should measure 4 ft wide. What is the area of the walkway?

320 ft²

Grade 5   21   Chapter 14

14-3

Name _____ Date _____

Homework Practice
Areas of Rectangles

Find the area of each rectangle.

1.
2 cm
4 cm

8 cm²

2.
40 mm
15 mm

600 mm²

3.
4 in.
4 in.

16 in.²

4. rectangle
$\ell = 3$ yd
$w = 4$ yd

12 yd²

5. rectangle
$\ell = 4$ in.
$W = 5$ in.

20 in.²

6. rectangle
$\ell = 32$ mm
$w = 46$ mm

1,472 mm²

Find the unknown width.

7. rectangle
$\ell = 3$ in.
$A = 6$ square inches
$w =$ **2 in.**

8. rectangle
$\ell = 45$ mm
$A = 3,150$ square millimeters
$w =$ **70 mm**

Spiral Review

Solve.

9. Mike's room is 12 feet by 15 feet. How many square feet of carpeting does he need to cover the entire floor?

180 ft²

10. Helen is planting tomatoes in her garden. She can place 3 plants per square foot. How many plants does she need if her garden measures 7 ft by 6 ft?

126 plants

Grade 5   20   Chapter 14

Grade 5   **A8**   *Chapter 14*

14-4

Name _____ Date _____

Reteach

Geometry: Three-Dimensional Figures

Prisms are three-dimensional figures. Their parts have special names.

face
edge
vertex

Face: flat surface on a prism or pyramid
Edge: segment where 2 faces meet
Vertex: point where edges meet
Prisms can be named by the shape of their bases.

6 faces
12 edges
8 vertices

The bases are rectangular.
This prism is a rectangular prism.

Describe parts of each figure that are parallel and congruent. Then identify the figure.

1. Triangular bases are congruent and parallel. Two rectangular sides are congruent. Triangular prism.

2. Opposite sides are parallel and congruent. Opposite edges are parallel and congruent. Rectangular prism.

3. No parts are parallel or congruent. Cone.

4. The circular bases are parallel and congruent. Cylinder.

14-3

Name _____ Date _____

Enrich

Areas of Polygons

Graph the ordered pairs. Connect the points.
Record the length, width, and area of the rectangle.

1. (2, 3), (2, 7), (9, 3), (9, 7)

$l = $ **7** $w = $ **4** $A = $ **28**

2. (2, 1), (2, 8), (7, 1), (7, 8)

$l = $ **5** $w = $ **7** $A = $ **35**

3. (6, 1), (6, 6), (1, 1), (1, 6)

$l = $ **5** $w = $ **5** $A = $ **25**

4. (9, 8), (9, 1), (1, 1), (1, 8)

$l = $ **8** $w = $ **7** $A = $ **56**

Compare the length and width of each rectangle to the coordinates you graphed.

The length of each rectangle is equal to the difference of the second (y) coordinates.

The width of each rectangle is equal to the difference of the first (x) coordinates.

Answers (Lesson 14–4)

Skills Practice

Name _____ Date _____

14–4

Geometry: Three-Dimensional Figures

Describe parts of each figure that are parallel and congruent. Then identify the figure.

1.
The circular bases are parallel and congruent. **Cylinder.**

2.
The triangle bases are parallel and congruent. **Triangular prism.**

3.
Opposite edges are parallel and congruent. Opposite sides are parallel and congruent. Rectangular prism.

Describe parts of each figure that are perpendicular and congruent. Then identify the figure.

4.
No parts are perpendicular or congruent. **Cone.**

5.
The circular bases are congruent. They are perpendicular to the curved surface of the figure. **Cylinder.**

6.
The triangular bases are congruent. They are perpendicular to the rectangular faces. **Triangular prism.**

Solve.

7. Describe the number of faces, vertices and edges in a can of soup. Identify the shape of the can.

A can of soup has 2 faces, no edges, and no vertices. It is a cylinder.

Grade 5   24   Chapter 14

Homework Practice

Name _____ Date _____

14–4

Geometry: Three-Dimensional Figures

Describe parts of each figure that are perpendicular and congruent. Then identify the figure.

1.
face
edge
vertex

2.

Opposite faces are congruent. Opposite edges are congruent. Adjacent faces are perpendicular. Adjacent edges are perpendicular. Rectangular prism.

All faces are congruent. All edges are congruent. Adjacent faces are perpendicular. Adjacent edges are perpendicular. Rectangular prism.

3.

The circular bases are congruent and are perpendicular to the curved surface of the figure. Cylinder.

Spiral Review

Find the area of each rectangle.   (Lesson 14–3)

4.
13 in.
4 in.
52 in^2

5.
63 cm
17 cm
1,071 cm^2

6.
29 m
29 m
841 m^2

Grade 5   25   Chapter 14

14–4 Enrich

Name _____ Date _____

Three-Dimensional Figures

Complete the table for these three-dimensional shapes.

Figure	Number of Faces	Number of Vertices	Total Faces and Vertices	Number of Edges
A	6	8	14	12
B	5	6	11	9
C	7	10	17	15
D	8	12	20	18
E	5	5	10	8
F	7	7	14	12
G	9	9	18	16
H	8	6	14	12

Look for a pattern in the table above. Then complete this statement.

The sum of the number of faces and vertices is equal to the number of

edges _____ plus _____**2**_____ .

Let f = number of faces, v = number of vertices, and e = number of edges.
Write the statement you completed above as an equation.

$f + v = e + 2$

Write a formula for the number of edges.

$e = f + v - 2$

14–4 Problem-Solving Practice

Name _____ Date _____

Geometry: Three-Dimensional Figures

Solve.

1. Ricardo made a simple drawing of his house. It is a polyhedron with 6 faces. Four faces are rectangular, and 2 are square. What kind of figure is it?

   rectangular prism

2. Diane bought a can of soda. What kind of figure is the can?

   cylinder

3. Gary is playing a board game. When it is his turn, he tosses a kind of polyhedron that is used in many board games. What kind of polyhedron is it?

   cube

4. When Ben bought a poster, the salesperson placed it in a tube to protect it. What kind of shape is the tube?

   cylinder

   If the tube is slit down its side and laid flat, what shape would it make?

   rectangle

5. Describe the shape of a rectangular pyramid. How does it compare to a triangular prism?

   The base is a rectangle and the sides are triangles; the triangular prism has a top and bottom base that are triangles whereas the rectangular pyramid has only one base and a point at the top.

6. What kind of shape is a funnel? Describe the number of faces and vertices it has.

   cone; it has one face and one vertex.

   How many faces, edges, and vertices does it have?

   6 faces, 12 edges, 8 vertices

Answers

Page 28 (Reteach)

14–5

Reteach

Problem-Solving Strategy

Make a Model

Solve. Use the *make a model* strategy.

Pedro is laying out tiles for a design in his bathroom. The area is 20 inches by 16 inches, and the tiles are 2 inch squares. How many square tiles are needed to fill the area?

Step 1 Understand	**Be sure you understand the problem.** Pedro is laying 2-inch tile in a 20-inch by 16-inch area.
Step 2 Plan	**Make a plan.** You can use a piece of construction paper and small square pieces of paper to represent the tiles.
Step 3 Solve	**Carry out your plan.** Make a model of the area by measuring out a 20″ × 16″ rectangle on construction paper. 20 in. / 16 in. Cut out 2-inch squares from another piece of paper. Cover the 20″ × 16″ area completely with the squares. It will take 80 squares or tiles.
Step 4 Check	**Is the solution reasonable?** Reread the problem. Calculate to check your answer. Find the area of 20″ × 16″. It is 320 square inches. Each 2 inch tile has an area of 2″ × 2″ = 4 square inches. 320 square inches ÷ 4 square inches = 80 tiles

Make a model using paper to find the number of tiles needed.

Page 29 (Reteaching)

14–5

Reteaching

Problem-Solving Strategy (continued)

Solve. Use the *make a model* strategy.

1. Hugo is making a block tower. Each block is a 4-inch square and is 1 inch thick. If he has 35 blocks, what is the tallest height he can make with the blocks?

   140 inches

2. Susan wants to organize her bookshelf in her bedroom. It measures 36 inches long, and there are three shelves. If she has 25 two-inch wide books, 15 three-inch wide books, and 32 one-inch wide books, will she be able to fit them on the three shelves? If not, how many of each book will not fit?

   No, 19 inches of book width will not fit; Sample answer: 9 of the two-inch and 1 of the one-inch books will not fit

3. Patricia is making a clay game board. Each square needs to be 2 inches. If the board will be 16 inches square, how many total squares will it have?

   64

4. Pablo has a sheet of stickers that is 11 inches long. Each sticker is a 1 inch circle and there are 10 in each row. How many stickers are there on one page?

   110

5. Charo is making a picture frame with shells she found. Each shell is 2 inches long. If she makes a rectangular frame out of 20 shells, how large can she make the frame?

   Sample answer: 14 in by 6 in

14-5

Name _____ Date _____

Skills Practice
Problem-Solving Strategy

Solve. Use the *make a model* strategy.

1. Ping and Kuri are designing a small end table using 1-inch tiles. If Kuri picks three times as many tiles out than Ping, and Ping picks out 24 tiles, how many total tiles are there? The area of the table is 19 inches by 5 inches. Will they have enough tiles to cover the tabletop?

96 tiles; yes

2. The Miller family is redoing their garden. If they have a garden that is 500 square feet, and one side is 10 feet long, what is the length of the other side of the garden? If they plant 5 trees that need to be 5 feet apart and 5 feet away from the fence around the garden, will they have the space?

50 feet; yes

3. Bob is organizing his pantry. If he has cracker boxes that measure 12 inches high, 2 inches wide, and 10 inches long, how many boxes can he fit on a 24-inch-long shelf that is 14 inches deep?

16 boxes

4. You are packing picnic baskets for a day camp. Each basket needs to carry 8 square sandwiches, 8 apples, and 8 juice boxes. Would the best basket be an 18″ × 15″ × 9″ basket, a 72″ × 40″ × 18″ basket, or a 12″ × 6″ × 8″ basket?

18″ × 15″ × 9″

5. Roberto wants to build a long train track. If each piece of track is 6 inches long, and he has 42 pieces, can he make a track that is 20 feet long? Can he make a track that is 22 feet long?

yes; no

14-5

Name _____ Date _____

Homework Practice
Problem-Solving Strategy

Solve. Use the *make a model* strategy.

1. Nan and Sato are designing a coffee table using 4 inch tiles. Nan uses 30 tiles and Sato uses half as many. How many total tiles did they use? If the area of the table is 36 inches by 24 inches, will they have enough tiles for the table? If not, how many more will they need?

45 tiles; no; 9 more tiles

2. The Jones family is landscaping their yard. If they have a yard that is 160 square feet, and one side is 10 feet long, what is the length of the other side of the garden? If they plant 3 bushes that need to be 3 feet apart and 3 feet away from the fence around the yard, will they have the space?

16 feet; yes

3. Bob is organizing his closet. If he has clothing bins that measure 20 inches high, 18 inches wide, and 14 inches long, how many bins can he fit in a 60-inch long closet that is 30 inches deep and 72 inches high?

18 bins

4. Roberto wants to build a brick wall. Each brick layer is 3 inches thick, and the wall will be 18 inches tall. How many layers will it have?

6 layers

Spiral Review
Identify each figure. (Lesson 14–4)

5. This polyhedron has six rectangular faces. **rectangular prism**

6. This prism has triangular bases. **triangular prism**

7. This is a solid that has a circular base and one curved surface from the base to a vertex. **cone**

Answers

Answers (Lessons 14–5 and 14–6)

14–6

Name _____ Date _____

Reteach
Volume of Prisms

Volume is the amount of space a three-dimensional figure encloses. To find the volume of a rectangular prism, you can use a formula.

Find the volume of the rectangular prism. Use the formula $V = \ell wh$, where V = volume, ℓ = length, w = width, and h = height.

$V = \ell wh$
$V = 4 \times 3 \times 5$
$V = 60$ cubic units

height (h)
length (ℓ)
width (w)

Find the volume of each prism.

1.
$\ell = \underline{6}$ units
$w = \underline{3}$ units
$h = \underline{2}$ units
$V = \ell wh$
$V = \underline{6} \times \underline{3} \times \underline{2}$
$V = \underline{36}$ cubic units

2.
$\ell = \underline{3}$ units
$w = \underline{3}$ units
$h = \underline{3}$ units
$V = \ell wh$
$V = \underline{3} \times \underline{3} \times \underline{3}$
$V = \underline{27}$ cubic units

3.
$\ell = \underline{5}$ units
$w = \underline{4}$ units
$h = \underline{3}$ units
$V = \ell wh$
$V = \underline{5} \times \underline{4} \times \underline{3}$
$V = \underline{60}$ cubic units

14–5

Name _____ Date _____

Enrich
Follow Directions

Follow the directions to solve the problem. You may use cubes.

The rectangular prism to the right is made of 1-inch cubes. The prism is 2 inches wide by 4 inches long by 3 inches high.

1. What is the total surface area of the prism?

    52 in²

2. Label the front layer of cubes. Use the capital letters *A* through *D* to label the cubes in the first row, *E* through *H* to label the cubes in the second row, and *I* through *L* to label the cubes in the third row. Then draw a diagram that would show what the figure would look like if you removed cube *D*. How would the surface area of the cube change if you removed cube *D*?

    It would not change. Three surfaces were lost, but 3 were exposed.

3. Draw a model that shows what the figure would look like if you removed cube *C*. How would the surface area of the cube change if you removed cube *C*?

    It would increase by 2 square inches. Two surfaces were lost, but 4 were exposed.

4. Name a cube that could be removed to give a surface area of 56 square inches.

    For G

5. Cube *a* is behind cube *A*, cube *b* is behind cube *B*, cube *d* is behind cube *D*, and so on. Name a pair of cubes that could be removed to give a surface area of 50 square inches.

    A and *a*, or D and *d*, or I and *i*, or, L and *l*.

Answers (Lesson 14–6)

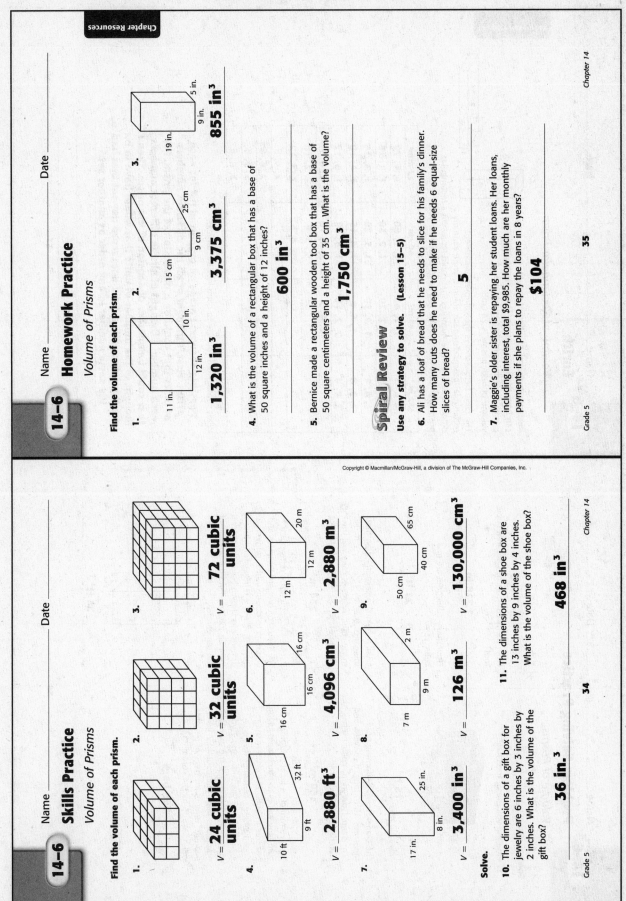

14–6 Homework Practice

Name _____ Date _____

Volume of Prisms

Find the volume of each prism.

1.

12 in.
11 in.
10 in.

1,320 in³

2.

15 cm
9 cm
25 cm

3,375 cm³

3.

19 in.
9 in.
5 in.

855 in³

4. What is the volume of a rectangular box that has a base of 50 square inches and a height of 12 inches?

600 in³

5. Bernice made a rectangular wooden tool box that has a base of 50 square centimeters and a height of 35 cm. What is the volume?

1,750 cm³

Spiral Review   (Lesson 15–5)

Use any strategy to solve.

6. Ali has a loaf of bread that he needs to slice for his family's dinner. How many cuts does he need to make if he needs 6 equal-size slices of bread?

5

7. Maggie's older sister is repaying her student loans. Her loans, including interest, total $9,985. How much are her monthly payments if she plans to repay the loans in 8 years?

$104

Grade 5   35   Chapter 14

14–6 Skills Practice

Name _____ Date _____

Volume of Prisms

Find the volume of each prism.

1.

v = **24 cubic units**

2.

v = **32 cubic units**

3.

72 cubic units

4.

9 ft
10 ft
32 ft

v = **2,880 ft³**

5.

16 cm
16 cm
16 cm

v = **4,096 cm³**

6.

12 m
12 m
20 m

v = **2,880 m³**

7.

8 in.
17 in.
25 in.

v = **3,400 in³**

8.

7 m
9 m
2 m

v = **126 m³**

9.

50 cm
40 cm
65 cm

v = **130,000 cm³**

Solve.

10. The dimensions of a gift box for jewelry are 6 inches by 3 inches by 2 inches. What is the volume of the gift box?

36 in.³

11. The dimensions of a shoe box are 13 inches by 9 inches by 4 inches. What is the volume of the shoe box?

468 in³

Grade 5   34   Chapter 14

14-6 Problem-Solving Practice
Volume of Prisms

Name _____ Date _____

Solve.

1. Find the volume of the chest.

2 ft, 4 ft, 2 ft

16 ft³

2. How many cubic inches are in a cubic foot?

1,728 in³

How many cubic feet are in a cubic yard?

27 ft³

3. The Donaldson's swimming pool measures 15 m long, 8 m wide, and 3 m deep. How many cubic meters of water will the pool hold?

360 m³

4. Myra is baking a cake in a pan that measures 9 in. by 13 in. by 2 in. How many cubic inches of cake will the pan hold?

234 in³

5. To save money, a local shipping company wants to purchase packing peanuts in bulk. The plant manager built a storage container that is 4 yds long, 10 yds wide, and 2 yds tall to store the peanuts. If the manager purchases bags that contain 7 ft³ of peanuts, how many bags of peanuts will it take to fill the container?

309 bags

6. Paul is shopping for a refrigerator. He needs to compare the sizes and volumes to decide which refrigerator to buy. He needs a refrigerator with the dimensions shown below in order to fit in his kitchen. Find the volume of the refrigerator.

6 ft, 2 ft, 2 ft

24 ft³

14-6 Enrich
Volume of Rectangular Prism

Name _____ Date _____

Rectangular prisms of different shapes can have the same volume. These rectangular prisms have different shapes, but the volume of both prisms is 24 cm³.

The table below shows the volumes of different rectangular prisms. For each volume, write as many different sets of three numbers that could represent a rectangular prism with that volume. One has been started for you.

32 in.³	40 m³	60 cm³	72 mm³
1, 1, 32	1, 1, 40	1, 1, 60	1, 1, 72
1, 2, 16	1, 2, 20	1, 2, 30	1, 2, 36
1, 4, 8	1, 4, 10	1, 3, 20	1, 3, 24
2, 2, 8	1, 5, 8	1, 4, 15	1, 4, 18
2, 4, 4	2, 2, 10	1, 5, 12	1, 6, 12
	2, 4, 5	2, 3, 10	1, 8, 9
		2, 5, 6	2, 2, 18
		3, 4, 5	2, 3, 12
			2, 4, 9
			2, 6, 6
			3, 3, 8
			3, 4, 6

What strategy did you use to complete the table?

Possible answer: I made an organized list for each prism. First, I thought of all the different numbers of units that could be a dimension of the prism. For each number, I thought of all the different numbers that could be another dimension of the prism. Then I thought of the number of units that would have to be the third dimension. I did not record any set that had the same number in any order as another set.

Skills Practice — 14-7

Name _____ Date _____

Skills Practice

Surface Areas of Prisms

Find the surface area of each rectangular prism.

1. **148 square units**

2. **136 square units**

3. (11 in., 12 in., 10 in.) **724 in.²**

4. (15 cm, 9 cm, 25 cm) **1,470 cm²**

5. (16 cm, 16 cm) **1,536 cm²**

6. (20 cm, 10 cm, 5.2 cm) **712 cm²**

7. (3 in., 3 in., 10 in.) **138 in.²**

8. (1.5 m, 2 m, 0.9 m) **12.3 m²**

Problem Solving Solve.

9. What is the surface area of a cardboard shipping box that is 26 inches long, 26 inches wide, and 18 inches high? **3,224 in.²**

10. What is the surface area of a 9-centimeter cube? **486 cm²**

Grade 5   39   *Chapter 14*

Reteach — 14-7

Name _____ Date _____

Reteach

Surface Areas of Prisms

You can find the **surface area** of a rectangular prism by finding the total area of all its faces. Each face is a rectangle, so use the formula $A = lw$ to find the area of each face.

Find the surface area of this rectangular prism.

Front face:	$5 \times 5 =$	25 square units
Back face:	$5 \times 5 =$	25 square units
Top face:	$5 \times 6 =$	30 square units
Bottom face:	$5 \times 6 =$	30 square units
Right face:	$5 \times 6 =$	30 square units
Left face:	$5 \times 6 =$	30 square units
Total surface area:		170 square units

Find the surface area of each rectangular prism.

1.

Front face:	$3 \times 4 =$	12 square units
Back face:	$3 \times 4 =$	12 square units
Top face:	$3 \times 5 =$	15 square units
Bottom face:	$3 \times 5 =$	15 square units
Right face:	$5 \times 4 =$	20 square units
Left face:	$5 \times 4 =$	20 square units
Total surface area:		94 square units

2.

Front face:	$7 \times 12 =$	84 cm²
Back face:	$7 \times 12 =$	84 cm²
Top face:	$7 \times 15 =$	105 cm²
Bottom face:	$7 \times 15 =$	105 cm²
Right face:	$15 \times 12 =$	180 cm²
Left face:	$15 \times 12 =$	180 cm²
Total surface area:		738 cm²

Grade 5   38   *Chapter 14*

Answers

Answers (Lesson 14–7)

14–7

Name _____ Date _____

Problem-Solving Practice

Surface Areas of Prisms

Solve.

1. Dylan has a toy box he wants to paint. He needs to find the surface area of the box in order to determine how much paint to buy. What is the surface area of the toy box?

2 ft 3 ft 4 ft

52 ft²

2. Jose is moving to a new house and has several packing boxes that are 2 ft by 2 ft by 3 ft. What is the surface area of each box?

32 ft²

3. Julia has a music box that she wants to cover with fabric. How many square inches of fabric will she need to cover the music box?

4 in. 5 in. 6 in.

148 in.²

4. Lenny builds kitchen cabinets that measure 3 ft tall, 1.5 ft long, and 2 ft deep. What is the surface area of each cabinet?

27 ft²

5. Lenny installs one of his cabinets from Problem 4 in a corner, attached to the ceiling. What is the surface area of the exposed faces?

13.5 ft²

6. Lenny installs two of his cabinets, side-by-side on a wall, attached to the ceiling. What is the surface area of the exposed faces?

27 ft²

14–7

Name _____ Date _____

Homework Practice

Surface Areas of Prisms

The **surface area** (*SA*) of a 3-dimensional figure is the sum of the area of all its faces.

A rectangular prism has 6 faces.

4 in. 2 in. 3 in.

Unfold the prism to examine the 6 faces.

	top 2		
2	3	2	3
left	front	right	back
4	4	4	4
2	bottom 2		3

Find the area of each of the 6 faces, and add.

Face	Area	In.²
front	3 × 4	12
back	3 × 4	12
top	3 × 2	6
bottom	3 × 2	6
left	2 × 4	8
right	2 × 4	8
	Total	52

Find the surface area of each figure.

1.
6 cm 3 cm 4 cm

108 cm²

2.
3 cm 3 cm 3 cm

54 cm²

3.
10 cm 3 cm 2 cm

The surface area of this rectangular prism is 52 in.²

112 cm²

6.
15 cm 6 cm 3 cm

270 cm²

Spiral Review

Find the volume of each prism. (Lesson 14–6)

4.
5 ft 5 ft 5 ft

125 ft³

5.
6 in. 3 in. 2 in.

36 in²

14-8 Reteach

Select Appropriate Measurement Formulas

Mr. Gonzalez wants to enclose a field for his horse. The field is 20 feet wide and 40 feet long. How much fencing will Mr. Gonzalez need? Should he find the perimeter or area of the field? Solve the problem.

The field is 20 feet by 40 feet.
You need to find how much fencing is needed.

Draw a diagram of the field. Label the length of each side.

20 ft

40 ft

Think: **Perimeter** is the distance around a closed figure. $P = 2\ell + 2w$
Area is the number of square units inside a closed figure. $A = \ell w$
Volume is the space enclosed by a figure. $V = \ell w h$

You need to find the **perimeter**, or the distance around the field.
Perimeter = 2 × (length + width) = 2 × (40 + 20)

Mr. Gonzalez needs 120 feet of fencing.

Determine whether you need to find the perimeter, area, or volume. Then solve.

1. A rectangular banner is 4 feet wide and 8 feet long. How much ribbon is needed to trim the borders of the banner?

   24 ft, perimeter

2. The floor of a room needs new carpet. The room is 10 feet wide and 12 feet long. How much carpet is needed to cover the floor?

   120 ft², area

14-7 Enrich

Surface Areas of Prisms

Suppose that your job is to design boxes for a gift manufacturer. You know the name of an item and its dimensions. Your job is to draw a box to fit the item. Then you have to draw its corresponding net. You need to label the dimensions on the box and net and tell the surface area of the box. When designing a box, you also need to follow these guidelines:

- Boxes must be rectangular prisms.
- Boxes should be as small as possible.
- The dimensions of each box must be in whole numbers of inches to allow room for packing materials.
- You do not have to be concerned about sides of the boxes overlapping.

Design a box for each item.

Item 1: A pottery giraffe that is $11\frac{1}{2}$ in. tall, $5\frac{1}{4}$ in. long, and $2\frac{5}{8}$ in. wide

Box

12 in.   6 in.   3 in.

Net

12 in.

6 in.   3 in.   6 in.

6 in.

6 in.

3 in.

Surface area: **252 in.²**

Item 2: A pyramid-shaped paperweight $4\frac{5}{8}$ in. tall with a $3\frac{3}{4}$ in. square base

Box

5 in.   4 in.   4 in.

Net

5 in.

4 in.   4 in.   4 in.

4 in.

4 in.

Surface area: **112 in.²**

Answers

Name _____ Date _____

14–8

Homework Practice

Select Appropriate Measurement Formulas

Determine whether you need to find the perimeter, area, or volume.
Then solve.

1. Charlene is filling a box planter with soil. Each bag of soil contains enough to fill 500 cubic inches. If the base of the box planter is a 9-inch square and the sides are 18 inches tall, how many bags of soil will Charlene need?

volume; 3 bags of soil

2. Tobias is helping his uncle paint the side of a barn. Each can of paint covers 80 square feet. If the side of the barn is 10 feet high and 15 feet wide, how many cans of paint will Tobias need?

area; 2 cans of paint

3. Gina is tying up a stack of newspapers with string. She wants the string to wrap around twice, once lengthwise and once crosswise. If the stack of newspapers is 11 inches wide, 13 inches long, and 15 inches high, how much string will she need?

perimeter; 108 inches, plus enough for the knot

Spiral Review

Find the surface area of each prism. (Lesson 14–7)

4.

1,470 cm²

5.

712 cm²

6.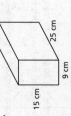

724 in.²

Grade 5   45   Chapter 14

Name _____ Date _____

14–8

Skills Practice

Select Appropriate Measurement Formulas

Determine whether you need to find the perimeter, area, or volume. Then solve.

1. Hayden wants to make a rectangular herb garden that is 4 feet long and 3 feet wide. She wants to plant lavender in half of the garden. How much of the garden will be covered with lavender?

Find the area of half of the garden; 6 square feet of lavender.

2. Daniel wants to plant a row of marigolds along the border of his vegetable garden. The garden is 6 feet long and 4 feet wide. How much of the garden will need to be covered with marigolds?

Find the perimeter; the border is 20 feet long.

3. Ms. Carmichael is building a deck with two levels. The lower level is a square. The length of each side is 5 feet. The upper level is rectangular in shape, 12 feet long and 8 feet wide. How much wood will she need to construct each level?

Find the area of each level; area of the lower level is 25 square feet, area of the upper level is 96 square feet, total area is 121 square feet.

4. Ms. Carmichael wants to use the space underneath the lower level as storage space. If the lower level of the deck is 4 feet high off the ground, how much storage space will she have?

100 cubic feet; volume

5. Jamison has 70 square feet of plywood to make a floor for a two-room clubhouse he is building. The floor of one room is 8 feet long and 6 feet wide. The floor of the other room is 5 feet long and 4 feet wide. How can he decide if he has enough plywood?

Find the area of both rooms; total area is 68 square feet, which is less than 70 square feet; he has enough plywood.

6. Amy wants to make a frame for a painting that is 24 inches long and 18 inches wide. She found a wood molding she would like to use. How can she decide how much molding she needs to make the frame?

Find the perimeter; 84 inches.

Grade 5   44   Chapter 14

14-8 Enrich

Name _____ Date _____

Chapter Resources

Choose an Appropriate Tool and Unit

Solve.

1. A punch is made from 3 pints of orange juice and 1 pint of lemonade.

   a. Will the punch fit in a punch bowl with a capacity of 2 quarts? Explain.

   Yes, 4 pt = 2 qt

   b. Will the punch fit in a bowl with a capacity of 7 cups? Explain.

   No, 4 pt = 8 c and 8 c > 7 c

2. A box is $9\frac{1}{2}$ inches long, $6\frac{3}{4}$ inches wide, and $2\frac{5}{8}$ inches deep.

   a. Will a model that is $1\frac{1}{2}$ inches tall, $6\frac{5}{8}$ inches wide, and $9\frac{3}{16}$ inches long fit inside the box? Explain.

   Yes, $1\frac{1}{2}$ in. < $2\frac{5}{8}$ in.; $6\frac{5}{8}$ < $6\frac{3}{4}$ in.; $9\frac{3}{16}$ in. < $9\frac{1}{2}$ in.

   b. Will a model that is $2\frac{3}{4}$ inches tall, $9\frac{5}{8}$ inches long, and $6\frac{3}{4}$ inches wide fit inside the box? Explain.

   No, $9\frac{5}{8}$ in. > $9\frac{1}{2}$ in.

3. Luisa and Dolores are running in a 100-yard race.

   a. What is an appropriate unit of measurement and measurement tool to use to measure their race times? Explain.

   Sample answer: use a stopwatch to measure their times to the nearest hundredth of a second

   b. Is it likely that their race times will be recorded to the nearest minute? Explain.

   No, you need seconds to record the race.

4. A 7-year-old child visits a doctor for a checkup.

   a. What is an appropriate unit of measurement and measurement tool to use to measure the weight of the child? Explain.

   Sample answer: Pounds and scale; a 7-year old child's weight is likely to be measured in pounds.

   b. What is an appropriate unit of measurement and measurement tool to use to measure the height of the child? Explain.

   Sample answer: Nearest quarter of an inch and wall ruler; measuring the child's height to the nearest quarter of an inch is more accurate than to the nearest inch.

Grade 5   47

14-8 Problem-Solving Practice

Name _____ Date _____

Select Appropriate Measurement Formulas

Solve.

1. Rita measured her living room floor to determine how many 12 in. by 12 in. tiles she needs to buy. Should she find the area or perimeter of the floor?

   area

2. Nolan measured the 4 sides of his garden. His garden is 20 ft long and 10 ft wide. How much garden fencing will he need to place around his garden? Did you use area or perimeter to find your answer?

   60 ft; perimeter

3. Bobby measures a room that is 9 ft wide and 15 ft long. He needs to decide how much carpet to buy. How many square feet of carpeting does he need?

   135 ft²; area

4. Nan wants to fill a canister with raisins. Would she need to find the area, perimeter, or volume of the canister to determine the amount of raisins that will fit?

   volume

5. Reggie is planting vegetables in a rectangular garden. The space measures 12 ft by 5 ft. He figured out how many feet of fencing he would need to go around the garden. He then decides to double the area. Reggie digs another rectangle with the same measurements next to the first garden. To find the new length of fencing needed, he multiplied the first measurement by 2. Is this correct? Why?

   no; The middle edge is counted twice. It does not need to be counted at all because he won't put fencing in the middle of the garden.

6. Leah and Alison have bedrooms with the same area, but different dimensions. Leah's bedroom measures 9 ft wide, and has a length 7 ft longer than the width. What are the possible dimensions of Alison's bedroom? What is the difference between the perimeters of the 2 bedrooms?

   Answers will vary for the dimensions of Alison's room. Answers will vary for the difference between the perimeters. The area of each room should be 144 ft².

Grade 5   46

Answers (Lesson 14–9)

Left half

Name _____ Date _____

14–9

Reteach

Problem-Solving Investigation: Choose the Best Strategy

Alberto often goes along with his sister, Sonia, to videotape her soccer games. He records each $1\frac{1}{2}$ hour game. If she played 11 games, would Alberto be able to fit all her games on one DVD if each DVD holds 15 hours of video?

Step 1 Understand	**Be sure you understand the problem.** Alberto will videotape Sonia's soccer games. Each game is $1\frac{1}{2}$ hours. Sonia played 11 games. The DVD will hold 15 hours of video.
Step 2 Plan • Make a model • Draw a diagram • Look for a pattern	**Make a plan.** Choose a strategy. You can draw a diagram. Draw a line segment that is 15 inches long. Then mark intervals that are $1\frac{1}{2}$ inches long. Count the intervals to see whether you have 11 intervals.
Step 3 Solve	**Carry out your plan.** Two games take 3 hours. So, in 15 hours Alberto can fit 2 × 5 or 10 games on his DVD. So 11 games will *not* fit on one DVD.
Step 4 Check	**Is the solution reasonable?** Reread the problem. How can you check your answers?

Right half

Name _____ Date _____

14–9

Reteach

Problem-Solving Investigation: Choose the Best Strategy
(continued)

Use any strategy shown below to solve each problem.

• Make a model   • Draw a diagram   • Look for a pattern   • Use logical reasoning

1. Mitchell spent some money on his haircut. He paid the cashier three $5-bills. He received $4.25 back from the cashier. How much did he pay for the haircut?

   $10.75

2. Callie is throwing a party and spends a total of $135. She spends $20 on cake, $40 on food, and $25 for decorations. If the rest of the money was spent on music, how much did the music cost?

   $50

3. Meredith spent $125 on new clothes. She also purchased school supplies that totaled $45. She received 10% back on her total purchase. How much did she receive back?

   $17.00

4. Jordan works at a pool during the week. Monday he worked for 30 minutes, Tuesday he worked for 40 minutes, Wednesday he worked for 50 minutes. If the pattern continues, how long will he work on Friday?

   One hour and 10 minutes

5. Roberto is looking for the better deal on a bag of pens. One bag has 6 pens for $3.65. Another bag is $4.98 for 8 pens. Which one should Roberto buy?

   $3.65 for 6 pens

Chapter Resources

14–9

Name _____ Date _____

Skills Practice

Problem-Solving Investigation: Choose the Best Strategy

Use any strategy shown below to solve each problem.

- Make a model
- Draw a diagram
- Look for a pattern
- Use logical reasoning

1. A pet store is building new cages for their birds. They have 8 cockatiels, 32 parakeets, and 28 finches. How many cages will they need if each cage will hold either 2 cockatiels, 10 parakeets, or 14 finches. The different types of birds are all kept separate.

10 cages

2. You decide to do an even exchange on an outfit that you received for your birthday. The top and pants total $32. If you pick another top for $14, how much is the highest price of the pants, that you can pick out?

$18.00

3. Danielle picks fruit from her family's lemon tree. She picked 28 lemons. If each lemon makes $\frac{1}{2}$ cup of lemonade after adding water, how many cups of lemonade can she make?

14 cups

4. Meredith is making a dress. She has 5 feet of ribbon. She needs 12 inches of ribbon for the neck and two 6-inch pieces for the cuffs. How many cuts will she need to make to get 6 equal lengths from the rest of the ribbon for bows?

5 cuts

5. Taye ran for 3 miles each week. On each fourth week, he ran an extra mile. How many miles did he run after 4 weeks? How many miles did he run after 7 weeks?

13 miles; 21 miles

Grade 5   50   Chapter 14

14–9

Name _____ Date _____

Homework Practice

Problem-Solving Investigation: Choose the Best Strategy

Use any strategy shown below to solve each problem.

- Make a model
- Draw a diagram
- Look for a pattern
- Use logical reasoning

1. The Humane Society is building new cages for their dogs and cats. They have 2 crews of workers building them. There are 28 dogs and 34 cats. All the animals are kept separate. The first crew can build a cage in 1 hour and the second crew, which is smaller, takes 2 hours to build a cage. How many hours will it take to build the cages using both crews if they do not take a break?

42 hours for 62 cages

2. You are shopping for some new clothes. You buy a shirt for $28 and a pair of dress shoes for $45. If you give the cashier a $100 bill, how much change will you get back?

$27.00

3. Marge needs to bake 8 dozen cookies for a bake sale. For each batch of cookies she needs $4\frac{1}{2}$ cups of flour. Each batch makes 2 dozen cookies. How much flour does she need?

18 cups

Spiral Review

Determine whether you need to find the perimeter, area, or volume. Then solve. (Lesson 14–8)

4. Mr. Bauer wants to enclose his rectangular garden with a fence. If the garden measures 12 feet by 9 feet, how many feet of fencing will he need to buy?

42 ft

5. Jameson has a storage bin that is the shape of a cube for his building blocks. If one side of the cube measures 2 feet, how many cubic feet of space does he have for storage?

volume; 8 ft³

Grade 5   51   Chapter 14

Answers

Answers (Lesson 14–9 and Vocabulary Test)

14

Name _____ Date _____

Vocabulary Test

Match each word to its definition. Write your answers on the lines provided.

1. A __prism__ is a polyhedron with two parallel congruent faces.

2. A __3-dimensional figure__ is a solid figure.

3. The distance around a shape or region is the __perimeter__.

4. A __polygon__ is a closed figure made up of line segments that do not cross each other.

5. __cubic units__ are units for measuring volume, such as a cubic inch or a cubic centimeter.

6. A __cone__ is a solid that has a circular base and one curved surface from the base to a vertex.

7. __area__ is the number of square units needed to cover the inside of a region or plane figure.

8. __rectangular prism__ is a three dimensional object in which all 6 faces are rectangular.

area

cone

cubic units

rectangular prism

polygon

prism

three-dimensional figure

perimeter

14–9

Name _____ Date _____

Enrich

Perimeter and Area Problem-Solving

Solve. Explain how you found your solution.

1. Nick builds the box shown at the right. The top of the box is mahogany. The sides and bottom are pine. How much mahogany does Nick use?
   80 in.²; found the area of the top of the box

2. Jenny's pool is surrounded by square tiles that are each 2 feet by 2 feet. She needs a cover for her pool. How many square feet must the cover be? Explain.
   360 ft²; found the length and width of the inside perimeter of the tiles; found the area of the pool by multiplying 30 × 12

   Each ☐ is 2 ft by 2 ft.

3. The park to the right is a field of grass with a diagonal path that is made of gravel. Workers have put gates at each end of the path. The rest of the park will be surrounded by a fence. How many meters of fencing are needed?
   66 m; found the perimeter of the park and subtracted 2 m for each gate

4. A garden covers 36 square feet. What is the least amount of fence that could be used to enclose a garden of this size?
   24 ft; used factors of 36 to find possible dimensions; found dimensions that gave the smallest perimeter

Answers (Oral Assessment)

Name _____ Date _____

14 Oral Assessment

Use construction paper to cut out 3 rectangles of different sizes and label them A–C. Use a ruler to measure the length and width in centimeters for each rectangle. Label each rectangle with its corresponding height and width.

Read each question aloud to the student. Then write the student's answers on the lines below the question.

1. What is the area and perimeter of the rectangle A?
   Answers will vary.

2. What is the area and perimeter of rectangle B?
   Answers will vary.

3. What is the area and perimeter of rectangle C?
   Answers will vary.

4. Explain your answers.
   I used the formulas for area and perimeter of rectangles.
   $A = \ell w$ and $P = 2\ell + 2w$.

5. Which rectangle has the smallest area and perimeter?
   Answers will vary.

6. Justify your answer.
   Student should compare the shapes' areas and perimeters and be able to select the shape with the smallest of each.

7. What rectangle would have the largest surface area if they all had a width of 1 inch?
   Answers will vary.

Copyright © Macmillan/McGraw-Hill, a division of The McGraw-Hill Companies, Inc.

Name _____ Date _____

14 Oral Assessment (continued)

Draw and label a parallelogram with a base of 8 inches and a height of 7 inches on the board.

Read each question aloud to the student. Then write the student's answer on the lines below the question.

8. How does the area of this parallelogram relate to the area of a rectangle with a length of 8 inches and a width of 7 inches?
   The areas are equal.

9. What is the area of the parallelogram?
   56 square inches

Draw and label a triangle with a base of 10 inches and a height of 6 inches on the board.

Read each question aloud to the student. Then write the student's answer on the lines below the question.

10. How does the area of a triangle relate to the area of a parallelogram?
    Since a parallelogram can be formed by two congruent triangles, the area of a triangle $= \frac{1}{2} bh.$

11. What is the area of the triangle?
    30 square inches

Assessment

Answers

Chapter 14 Assessment Answer Key

Chapter Diagnostic Test Page 54	Chapter Pretest Page 55	Quiz 1 Page 56
1. 30	1. 34 inches	1. 74 cm
2. 30	2. 52 feet	2. 34 in.
3. $13\frac{1}{2}$	3. 2 parallel, congruent faces; triangular prism	3. 11.6 m
4. 37.1		4. 16 cm
5. $57.98	4. 90 in.^{3}	5. 250 in.^{2}
6. 112		
7. 78	5. 1,320 in.^{3}	6. 52 in^2
8. 84		
9. 576		
10. 1,428	6. 130,000 cm^3	7. 7.5 cm^2
11. 48		
12. 168		
13. 252		8. 4 cm^2
14. $216	7. 126 m^3	

Chapter 14 Assessment Answer Key

Quiz 2
Page 57

1. 810 in^3

2. $1,500 \text{ in}^3$

3. 540 cm^3

4. $1,500 \text{ in}^3$

5. Opposite edges of the base are parallel. 4 triangle faces are congruent. Rectangular pyramid.

6. 12

7. yes

Quiz 3
Page 58

1. 550 cm^2

2. 990 cm^2

3. area; 100 square feet

4. perimeter; 322 inches

5. area; $1,120

6. $\dfrac{9}{20}$

7. 20 times; 480 times

Mid-Chapter Test
Page 59

1. 260 in.

2. 24 in.

3. 20 ft

4. 100 in.

5. 16 cm^2

6. 14 cm^2

7. 32 ft^2

8. 800 ft^2

Answers

Chapter 14 Assessment Answer Key

Form 1
Page 65

1. **B**

2. **G**

3. **C**

4. **G**

5. **D**

6. **H**

Page 66

7. **C**

8. **G**

9. **D**

10. **J**

11. **C**

12. **F**

13. **B**

14. **F**

Form 2A
Page 67

1. **A**

2. **H**

3. **D**

4. **G**

5. **D**

6. **112 in²**

(continued on the next page)

Chapter 14 Assessment Answer Key

7. B

8. H

9. B

10. J

11. C

12. J

13. C

14. F

1. C

2. H

3. C

4. G

5. C

6. B

7. B

8. **11.5 ft²**

9. A

10. F

11. A

12. B

13. A

14. G

Answers

Chapter 14 Assessment Answer Key

Form 2C
Page 71

1. _____ **160 m³** _____

2. _____ **none** _____

3. _____ **60 cubic units** _____

4. _____ **105 ft²** _____

5. _____ **30 m²** _____

6. _____ **24 ft²** _____

Page 72

7. _____ **63.5 m** _____

8. _____ **15.5 square units** _____

9. _____ **14 cm** _____

10. _____ **11 ft** _____

11. _____ **66 in.** _____

12. _____ **660 m³** _____

13. _____ **168 mi³** _____

14. _____ **445 ft²** _____

15. _____ **5,400 in²** _____

Form 2D
Page 73

1. _____ **66 in.** _____

2. _____ **11 ft** _____

3. _____ **14 cm** _____

4. _____ **63.5 m** _____

5. _____ **10 square units** _____

6. _____ **1,225 m²** _____

7. _____ **348 in²** _____

8. _____ **206 cm²** _____

9. _____ **96 cm²** _____

(continued on the next page)

Chapter 14 Assessment Answer Key

Form 2D (*continued*)
Page 74

10. _____ 54 m³ _____

11. _____ 160 m³ _____

12. _____ 224 mi³ _____

13. _____ **1 pair of parallel and congruent sides** _____

14. _____ 192 ft² _____

15. _____ perimeter _____

16. _____ 600 ft³ _____

17. _____ 13 ft² _____

Form 3
Page 75

1. _____ 12z cm² _____

2. _____ 1,470 cm² _____

3. _____ 22 ft² _____

4. _____ 18r ft² _____

5. _____ 1,260 cm³ _____

6. _____ 48 in³ _____

7. _____ 550 in² _____

Page 76

8. _____ **3 pairs of parallel and congruent sides** _____

9. _____ 23 square units _____

10. _____ 11 in. _____

11. _____ 9 in. _____

12. _____ *l* = 14 m, *w* = 12 m, *h* = 9 m _____

13. _____ 232 in² _____

Answers

Chapter 14 Assessment Answer Key

Level	Specific Criteria
4	The student demonstrates a **_thorough understanding_** of the mathematics concepts and/or procedures embodied in the task. The student has responded correctly to the task, used mathematically sound procedures, and provided clear and complete explanations and interpretations. The response may contain minor flaws that do not detract from the demonstration of a thorough understanding.
3	The student demonstrates an **_understanding_** of the mathematics concepts and/or procedures embodied in the task. The student's response to the task is essentially correct with the mathematical procedures used and the explanations and interpretations provided demonstrating an essential but less than thorough understanding. The response may contain minor errors that reflect inattentive execution of the mathematical procedures or indications of some misunderstanding of the underlying mathematics concepts and/or procedures.
2	The student has demonstrated only a **_partial understanding_** of the mathematics concepts and/or procedures embodied in the task. Although the student may have used the correct approach to obtaining a solution or may have provided a correct solution, the student's work lacks an essential understanding of the underlying mathematical concepts. The response contains errors related to misunderstanding important aspects of the task, misuse of mathematical procedures, or faulty interpretations of results.
1	The student has demonstrated a **_very limited understanding_** of the mathematics concepts and/or procedures embodied in the task. The student's response to the task is incomplete and exhibits many flaws. Although the student has addressed some of the conditions of the task, the student reached an inadequate conclusion and/or provided reasoning that was faulty or incomplete. The response exhibits many errors or may be incomplete.
0	The student has provided a **_completely incorrect_** solution or uninterpretable response, or no response at all.

Chapter 14 Assessment Answer Key

Page 72, Chapter Extended-Response Test
Sample Answers

In addition to the scoring rubric found on page A30, the following sample answers may be used as guidance in evaluating open-ended assessment items.

1. **a.** The number of tiles needed to cover a kitchen floor can be classified as area because the length and width of the floor will determine the number of tiles.

   b. The amount of sand in a sandbox can be classified as volume because you are measuring length, width, and height.

2. **a.** A lawn is a rectangle shape. The perimeter of a rectangle is the sum of the lengths and widths. It is also two times the length plus two times the width. In symbols: P = 2l + 2w. Using the dimensions of the lawn: P = 2(35 yds) + 2(10 yds). P = 90 yds. The perimeter of the lawn is 90 yards.

   b. The shape of a pennant is a triangle. The area of a triangle is one half the product of its base and its height. In symbols: $A = \frac{1}{2}bh$. Using the dimensions of the football pennant: $A = \frac{1}{2}$ (3 ft × 1.5 ft). A = 2.25 ft². The area of the pennant is 2.25 ft².

   c. The area of a rectangle is the product of any base and its height. In symbols: A = bh. Using the dimensions of the tile: A = 27 cm × 1.5 cm. A = 40.5 cm². The area of the tile is 40.5 cm².

3. **a.** Both the box of macaroni and the box of cereal are rectangular prisms.

The volume of a rectangular prism is the product of its length, width, and height. In symbols, V = lwh. Using the dimensions from the table, the volume of the box of macaroni is 13 × 8 × 20 = 2,080 cm³, and the volume of the box of cereal is 19 × 6 × 25 = 2,850 cm³. 2,850 cm³ > 2,080 cm³, so the box of cereal has more volume.

   b. The volume of a box of kosher salt is the product of its length, width, and height. Using the dimensions from the table, V = 12 × 5 × 16 = 960 cm³. Round the volume to 1,000 cm³ to estimate the number of boxes of kosher salt that can fit in the kitchen cabinet: 15,000 cm³ ÷ 1,000 cm³ = 15. About 15 boxes of kosher salt can fit in the kitchen cabinet.

   c. To find out how much wrapping paper is needed, determine the surface area of the box of green tea, which is a cube because the measuremets of its length, width, and height are all the same. The surface area of a cube is 6 times the square of the length of a side. In symbols, S = 6s². Using the dimensions from the table, S = 6 (10 cm)². S = 600 cm². Felicity will need 600 cm² of wrapping paper to wrap the box of green tea.

Answers

Chapter 14 Assessment Answer Key

Cumulative Test Practice Chapters 1–14

Page 78   **Page 79**   **Page 80**

2. **F**

6. **F**

3. **C**

7. **B**

4. **F**

8. **H**

9. **1,200 cu cm**

5. **D**

10. **588 ft³**

11. **16 ft²**

12. **1,000 mm**

1. **C**

13. **yes**